confident
aga
cooking

sarah whitaker

with photographs by

sam herbert

Food preparation:
Sarah Whitaker

Food styling:
Sarah Whitaker, Clementine Pickering and Sam Herbert
*(all the photographs are of the actual recipes and once we had finished,
we ate the lot!)*
Photographs:
Sam Herbert

There is probably no such thing as an original recipe. If I have inadvertently duplicated anyone else's ideas, I apologise – sometimes I think there must be a spy in my kitchen when I see a television cook make a dish that I thought I had invented the day before!

Details of demonstrations, further copies of this book
and copies of Sarah's other recipe collections:

Effortless Aga Cooking
Casual Aga Cooking
Relaxed Aga Cooking
and
The Twelve Days of Aga Christmas

are available from:
The Trout, Nether Wallop, Hampshire, SO20 8EW
Email: sarah@sarahwhitaker.com
www.sarahwhitaker.com
www.theagalady.com
twitter: @theagalady
facebook: theagalady

confident aga cooking

sarah whitaker
with photographs by
sam herbert

for Anthony, with love
Daisy, Clementine and James, with thanks for the suggestions and eating
and for
Penny Pickering

Published in Great Britain by Sarah Whitaker
The Trout, Nether Wallop, Stockbridge, Hampshire, SO20 8EW
www.sarahwhitaker.com
01264 781072

Photographs by Sam Herbert

contents

getting to know your aga

It is perfectly possible to cook on an Aga for many years and never use any of the cast iron cooking techniques. Lots of people do. They may wonder why the cooker loses heat so quickly, or will not brown the roast potatoes properly for Sunday lunch, but love the cooker so much that they don't mind, much. Then they learn a few simple techniques, keep the lids down and cook more in the ovens and – as if by magic – the cooker stops losing heat, the roast potatoes are crisp and they never look back.

If this is you, read on . . .

Life with an Aga is like a friendship. Its warm, benign presence in the kitchen is such a comfort in the house.

An Aga has two top plates: the left hand **boiling plate**, which is very hot – it boils. The right hand, **simmering plate**, is about half the temperature of the boiling plate – it simmers. The two-oven Aga has a top, **roasting oven,** which is very hot – it roasts, grills, bakes and fries, and a lower, **simmering oven** that is about half the temperature of the roasting oven – it simmers. The three-oven Aga also has a **baking oven** that runs at a perfect temperature for baking, about

half way between the roasting and simmering ovens, slightly hotter towards the top. The four-oven and five-oven Agas also have a **warming oven**, cooler than the simmering oven. And that's it.

A traditional Aga is a heat storage cooker, which maintains its heat until the lids are opened for too long or very cool food is put into the ovens, when the thermostat kicks in and the lost heat gradually regenerates. About 80% of all cooking on an Aga takes place in the oven, saving heat and fuel. This has the added benefit of no spitting fat to clear up and no cooking smells – the ovens are vented to the flue and all smells just disappear up the chimney.

Please don't turn the Aga up if you are cooking for a crowd – you will only burn things, as it will be much hotter than you are used to! It may cook a little more slowly if the ovens are very full, but it will be consistent and reliable.

If you have an Aga with the AIMS system, leave the computer to turn it up and down to the slumber mode to save fuel at night, but be aware that you should not cook in the ovens unless they are at full temperature.

The new generation of 21st century Agas, the Dual Control, Total Control and City60 are more economical and efficiently insulated. The ovens are pre-set to specific temperatures and cannot be adjusted.

The Dual Control is designed that the ovens are on all the time, just as with a traditional Aga, and the hotplates can be switched on and off as required, saving energy since you no longer need to keep the boiling plate hot 24 hours a day. It has an Eco setting where all the ovens drop in temperature to save energy.

In the Eco setting the roasting oven drops to around 180–190C, the baking oven to 150–140C and the simmering oven becomes a warming oven.

Aga do not recommend that raw meat is cooked in the Dual Control on its Eco setting, but it is perfect for reheating cooked food, steaming vegetables and baking cakes.

The Total Control and City60 are slightly different, in that the ovens are independently controlled and you can use one, any, or all of them at any time. Allow at least 45 minutes to an hour from switching on the cold cooker to putting anything into the oven, as the heat needs to saturate the cast iron ovens for it to perform properly.

The Total Control has a slumber setting, when the baking and roasting ovens drop to about 120C and the heat-up time from this setting is about 20 minutes.

It is not recommended that raw meat is cooked in the Total Control on the slumber setting, but it is perfect for slow cooked fruit cakes!

Many of these recipes refer to hanging the tins and shelves from the runners at the sides of the ovens. Always count the runners downwards from the top of the oven. Hanging roasting and baking tins from the runners uses less space – you can fit much more into the ovens at once!

In all these recipes, I have assumed that whichever model you have, the Aga is on, at full temperature and ready to cook.

a note about ingredients

I have deliberately not specified organic, free range or unrefined ingredients in my recipes. The choice is up to you, the cook.

I prefer to use good quality, seasonal, locally produced, fresh ingredients, rather than those imported from around the world, out of season and context.

I will not use any ingredient that I cannot buy easily close to home – it seems so unfair to say that a recipe will only work if you use particular herbs gathered by fairies in the Provençal moonlight or a certain brand of olive oil only available from one Italian delicatessen in a back street in Islington or through the internet!

I now use English cold pressed rapeseed oil in most of my recipes because it is so versatile and delicious and can be used for anything from a salad dressing to a stir fry. It is also local – almost everywhere in the UK there is a farmer growing rapeseed within 20 miles.

preparing ahead

In many of these recipes I indicate that food can be prepared ahead – to be cooked and either kept warm, or cooled and reheated to eat later or the next day.

Many of these dishes freeze really well, either part-cooked or ready to defrost and serve.

This does not mean that you have to make things in advance, just that you can if it suits you to do so.

hot and sour chicken noodle soup

To feed more people: Double the ingredients will feed up to 10, especially if served in small bowls

Serves 4 – 6

1 medium chicken

1 tbsp coriander seeds

2"/5cm piece fresh ginger

1 stalk lemongrass

3 pints (1.5 litres) water

1 lime

2 tbsp fish sauce (nam pla)

2 tbsp soy sauce

2 cloves garlic

2 red chillies

Bunch spring onions

1 sachet coconut cream

Pack uncooked rice noodles (300g)

2 tbsp chopped fresh coriander

Oven:

Boiling plate, simmering oven, 130C, 250F, Gas 1

Prepare in advance:

Soup will keep in the fridge for 24 hours

Prepare ahead:

Stock with meat in will keep warm for an hour in the simmering or warming oven, add the rest of the ingredients 2 minutes before serving

Freeze:

Stock with meat in will freeze, add the rest of the ingredients to the boiling soup 2 minutes before serving

1   Chop the ginger and bash the lemongrass stalk to release its flavour.

2   Put the chicken into a large casserole with the coriander seeds, ginger and lemongrass. Add 3 pints of water, cover and bring to the boil.

3   Move the pan of chicken to the simmering oven for an hour.

4   Once the chicken is cooked, take the pan from the oven and remove the chicken. Leave to cool, while you strain the stock into a new, clean pan.

5   Remove the chicken meat from the bones and shred into easy to eat pieces. Set the sachet of coconut cream onto the back of the Aga to soften.

6   Put the chicken meat into the pan of stock and bring back to the boil.

7   Trim and slice the spring onions, finely chop the garlic and chillies. Grate the rind from the lime and squeeze the juice. Add to the pan, with all the rest of the ingredients. Stir and serve after 2 minutes.

courgette and
pea soup

To feed more people: Serve in smaller bowls to 6 people, or make double for up to 15 servings

Serves 4 – 5

1 oz (25g) butter

1 tbsp rapeseed oil

2 large courgettes

1 onion

1 clove garlic

1½ lb (600g) peas

2 pints (1 litre) good stock

Handful fresh basil

Salt and pepper

¼ pint (150ml) cream

Basil leaves to serve

Oven:

Simmering oven, 130C, 250F, Gas 1

Prepare in advance:

Cooked, cooled soup will keep in the fridge for 24 hours

Prepare ahead:

Will keep warm in the simmering or warming oven for an hour

Freeze:

Yes

1 Peel and chop the onion, crush the garlic. Chop the courgettes. Set the stock in a jug on the back of the Aga to warm up.

2 Heat the butter and oil in a heavy based pan on the boiling plate, and add the onions. Cover with a lid and, when the lid is too hot to rest your hand on, transfer the pan to the simmering oven for 10 minutes until the onions are soft.

3 Move the pan to the simmering plate and stir in the courgettes and stir over the heat for a minute. Add the stock and bring to the boil, then add the peas. Cover and bring back to the boil, then transfer the pan back to the simmering oven for a further 10 minutes.

4 When the vegetables are all soft, add most of the basil leaves and whizz the soup until smooth. Season and serve, with a blob of cream and a basil leaf in each bowl.

Aga tip: The easiest way to serve a lot of soup is to transfer it to a jug and pour into the bowls. Put the cream and basil leaves into the bowls in advance, and the pouring soup will swirl the cream around the bowl

carrot and orange soup

To feed more people: Double the ingredients will feed up to 12, especially if you serve it in small bowls!

Serves 4

2 tbsp rapeseed oil

1 onion

4 medium carrots

2 sweet potatoes, about 12 oz (375g)

1 medium potato

1½ pints (800ml) stock

Salt and pepper

3 tbsp orange juice

3 tbsp double cream

1 tbsp chopped coriander

Oven:

Simmering oven, 130C, 250F, Gas 1

Prepare in advance:

Will keep in the fridge for 24 hours

Prepare ahead:

Will keep warm in the simmering or warming oven for an hour or so

Freeze:

Yes

1   Peel and chop the onion. Dice the carrots, sweet potatoes and potatoes.

2   Heat the oil in a large pan on the simmering plate, add all the vegetables. Cover and when the lid of the pan is too hot to rest your hand on, transfer to the simmering oven for about 20 minutes until the vegetables are soft.

3   Move the pan to the boiling plate, add the stock and bring the soup to the boil. It is now ready to liquidise and serve, or you can put it back into the simmering oven for up to an hour before whizzing.

4   Liquidise the soup and season well.

5   Stir in the orange juice, cream and coriander and serve with crusty bread.

smoked salmon taramasalata

Makes enough as a dip for several people, depending upon what they are dipping into it – bread does not go as far as vegetable chips!

3 slices of day old white bread

7 oz (200g) smoked salmon trimmings

1 clove garlic

½ onion

¼ pint (150ml) olive oil

5 tbsp fresh lemon juice

Salt and pepper

Oven:

None!

Prepare ahead:

Will keep in the fridge for a day or so

Freeze:

No

1 Soak the slices of bread briefly in a bowl of water. Squeeze out the excess water and set aside.

2 Put the salmon and onion into a processor or blender and whizz.

3 Tear the bread into pieces and add to processor and whizz again. With the machine running, dribble the olive oil into the mixture, forming a paste.

4 Add the lemon juice a bit at a time and blend until smooth and creamy. Season well.

5 Serve taramasalata with pitta triangles or other bread or vegetable for dipping.

duck liver pâté

Adding cream cheese to the pâté makes it milder

8 oz (225g) duck livers

8 oz (230g) butter

2 cloves garlic

Handful fresh tarragon

2 tbsp brandy

7 oz (200g tub) cream cheese

Oven:

Simmering plate; roasting oven, 200C 400F, Gas 1

Prepare ahead:

Will keep in the fridge for up to 48 hours

Freeze:

Yes

1   Set the pack of cream cheese onto the back of the Aga to warm and soften.

2   Peel and crush the garlic.

3   Melt the butter in a large pan on the simmering plate and add the livers and garlic. Cover the pan and set onto the floor of the roasting oven for about 20 minutes.

4   Remove from the oven and allow to cool.

5   Pour the cooked livers into a food processor and whizz until smooth. Add a handful of tarragon and the cream cheese and whizz again, until it is well incorporated.

6   Chill for about an hour, until thickened but not set.

Alternatives:

- Use the livers from the Christmas turkey to make pâté for Boxing day!
- Use chicken livers instead of duck

potted shrimps

I have seen packets of these tiny, delicately flavoured shrimps at several of the large supermarkets, they must be a new fad! A real treat, formerly only available near to Morecambe Bay in Lancashire where they are fished, potted shrimps are now here for everyone

To feed more people: Two packets of shrimps and 6 oz butter will feed up to 4, three packets of shrimps and a whole packet of butter will give decent helpings to 6 or 7 people. Or four really greedy happy people

Serves 2

  1 pack (90g) brown shrimps

  3 oz (865g) butter

  5 grates nutmeg

  Black pepper

Oven:

  Back of Aga

Prepare in advance:

  Will keep in the fridge for up to 48 hours

Freeze:

  Don't see why not! Just let it defrost thoroughly

1 Set the butter in a bowl on the back of the Aga to melt.

2 Open the pack of shrimps and tip them onto a piece of kitchen towel and pat dry.

3 Pile the shrimps into a bowl.

4 Grate the nutmeg into the melted butter and stir in a little pepper.

5 Pour the flavoured butter over the shrimps and refrigerate until the butter has set.

6 Serve at room temperature with fresh, warm bread.

warm tomato salad

To feed more people: Double the ingredients will stretch around 10, especially if served as part of a summer buffet

Serves 4

1 lb cherry tomatoes

1 tbsp rapeseed oil

1 tbsp balsamic vinegar

Salt and pepper

½ tsp sugar

Fresh basil leaves to finish

Oven:

Simmering oven, 130C, 250F, Gas 1

Prepare in advance:

The cooked tomatoes will keep in a jar in the fridge for 48 hours

Prepare ahead:

Leave the tomatoes in a bowl on the side of the Aga to keep warm for an hour or so

Freeze:

Yes, but not to eat as a salad afterwards, just to add to a casserole or similar

1   Line the small roasting tin with Bake-O-Glide.

2   Halve the tomatoes and tip into the small roasting tin. Add the oil and shake to coat all the tomatoes with the oil.

3   Put the tin into the simmering oven and bake for an hour until the tomatoes have shrunk a bit and their flavours have concentrated.

4   Take the tin from the oven and leave to cool for 10 minutes, then pour on the balsamic vinegar and seasonings.

5   Shake and serve warm or tepid with some basil leaves torn over them.

beetroot puffs

Makes 4 individual servings

2 large beetroot

7 oz (200g) tub cream cheese

2 tbsp horseradish sauce

2 oz cheddar cheese

2 eggs

4 oz (110g) plain flour

½ pint (300 ml) milk

Pinch of salt

3 tbsp sunflower oil or dripping

Oven:

Roasting oven, 220C, 450F, Gas 7

Prepare in advance:

Cooked, cooled puffs will keep in the fridge for 24 hours

Prepare ahead:

Remove cooked puffs from the oven, leave to cool and then reheat for 5 minutes before serving

Freeze:

Yes, reheat from frozen in the roasting oven for about 10 minutes

1 If using raw beetroot, put them, whole, into the roasting oven for about half an hour to cook. Remove from the oven and allow to cool before peeling them, then grate them.

2 Meanwhile, put the plain shelf into the roasting oven on the 3rd runners.

3 Set the packet of cream cheese onto the back of the Aga to soften.

4 Put a little oil into each hole of a 4–hole Yorkshire pudding tin and set it on top of the plain shelf in the oven.

5 Put the eggs, salt and flour into a wide jug and mix to a paste. Add the milk a little at a time, whisking until it is all incorporated.

6 Pour the batter into the hot tin and bake on top of the heated shelf for about 15 minutes.

7 While the batter is in the oven, mix together the grated beetroot, cream cheese and horseradish.

8 Pile the purple mixture onto the hot Yorkshire puddings and grate the cheese over them. Return to the oven for 5 minutes until the cheese is melted and bubbling.

Aga tip: Putting the plain shelf into the oven before cooking the puddings traps the heat above the shelf and raises the temperature for really puffy Yorkshires

spiced almonds

Serves 4

1 tbsp water

1 egg white

1 lb (450g) whole almonds

1 oz (25g) caster sugar

1 tsp salt

1 tsp smoked paprika

1 tsp ground cumin

1 tsp ground coriander

½ tsp chilli powder

Oven:

Simmering oven, 130C, 250F,

Gas 1

Prepare in advance:

Will keep in an airtight tin for up to

a week

Freeze:

Yes

Alternatives:

- Use mixed spice for Christmas flavoured almonds
- Use ground allspice for a different flavour
- Use cashews, pecans, groundnuts or hazelnuts instead of or as well as the almonds

1 Put the water and egg white into a bowl and whisk until foamy. Stir in the almonds and make sure that they are well coated in the egg mixture.

2 Tip the coated almonds into a colander to drain off excess liquid.

3 Mix together all the rest of the ingredients and stir in the almonds.

4 Line a large shallow roasting tin with Bake-O-Glide and tip the almonds into this. Shake so that they are in a single layer.

5 Bake for about an hour and a half, shaking the tin every half hour or so.

6 Serve cold.

jim's chilli dip and marinade

This is a really useful mixture, it can be served as a garlicky ketchup or barbecue sauce, added to cream cheese for a dip, served alone as a spicy dip, or rubbed into meat or chicken before grilling or roasting

4 large cloves garlic

1 tbsp cumin seeds

1 tbsp smoked paprika

1 red pepper

4 medium red chillies

2 slices white bread

1 tsp light muscovado sugar

4 tbsp white wine vinegar

10 tbsp rapeseed oil

Salt and pepper

Oven:

Roasting oven, 200C, 400F, Gas 6

Prepare in advance:

This improves if it is kept in the fridge for a day or two and it will keep in the fridge for up to a week

Freeze:

No

1. Put the garlic cloves and cumin seeds into a roasting tin and hang it from the 3rd runners in the roasting oven for about 10 minutes.

2. Heat the toaster on the boiling plate, then toast the bread until golden on both sides.

3. Wash the pepper and chillies and cut them into chunks, discarding the core and seeds. Peel the roasted garlic.

4. Pile the vegetables and spices into a processor. Add the bread, sugar and vinegar and whizz to a paste. With the motor running, pour the olive oil into the mixture. Season.

5. Pour into a bowl, cover and refrigerate for at least 12 hours for the flavours to develop.

6. Serve with chunks of bread or vegetables to dip in or use as a rub or marinade for meat or poultry.

Aga Tip: Heating the Aga toaster before you put any bread into it stops the bread from sticking as it toasts

me made in Nether Wallop

Jim's chilli dip
February 2015.

Sarah Whitaker
The Trout, Nether Wallop, Hampshire, SO20 NEW

red onion tatins

To feed more people: Double the ingredients will make 8 tarts, or using 6 smaller onions and 3 tbsp of red onion marmalade and a pack of pastry will make 12 using a muffin tin

Serves 4

2 red onions

2 tbsp red onion marmalade

½ pack ready rolled puff pastry

Oven:

Roasting oven, 200C, 400F, Gas 1

Prepare in advance:

Assembled tarts, with cold onions, will keep in the fridge for 24 hours

Prepare ahead:

Will keep warm in the simmering or warming oven for an hour

Freeze:

Yes, unbaked

1 Peel and halve the onions. Lay them into the small roasting tin, lined with Bake-O-Glide.

2 Hang the tin from the 3rd runners in the roasting oven for about 20 minutes until the onions have softened and browned.

3 Leave the onions to cool for 10 minutes.

4 Take a 4–hole Yorkshire pudding tin and set the onions into it, cut side down. Spread the red onion marmalade over the rounded side of the onions.

5 Unroll the pastry and lay it over the onions, if you want to have extra-large tarts, do not cut round each onion shape. If you want to have tidy tarts, use a biscuit cutter to cut neat circles of pastry and lay them over the onions.

6 Slide the grid shelf onto the 3rd runners in the roasting oven and set the Yorkshire pudding tin onto it. Bake for about 8–10 minutes until the pastry is golden and puffed up.

7 Turn out the tarts and serve with a little green salad.

aga rice

To feed more people: Double the quantity will feed up to 9, three times will feed 14

Serves 4

½ pint in a measuring jug (300ml) long grain rice

¾ pint (450ml) water

Oven:

Simmering oven, 130C, 250F, Gas 1

Prepare in advance:

Best eaten on the day it is cooked

Prepare ahead:

Will keep warm in the simmering or warming oven for an hour or so

Freeze:

Yes, but cool it down really quickly and reheat really thoroughly

1   Measure the rice and water into a pan.

2   Bring to the boil.

3   Cover and transfer to the simmering oven for 15 – 150 minutes.

4   Serve.

Aga tip:

The rice is cooked when it has absorbed all the water, which will happen in about 12–15 minutes, ie the time indicated on the packet

It will then sit in the pan in the oven until you need it – it cannot go soggy as there is a finite amount of water. It cannot dry out as the lid is on the pan containing the steam

braised celery

To feed more people: Double the quantity will feed up to 12 if served as a vegetable to accompany a meal

Serves 4

1 head celery

1 medium onion

1 clove garlic

1 medium carrot

1 tbsp rapeseed oil

¼ pint stock

2 tbsp dry white Vermouth

Salt and pepper

Oven:

Simmering oven, 130C, 250F, Gas 1

Prepare in advance:

Cooked, cooled celery will keep in the fridge for 24 hours

Prepare ahead:

Will keep warm in the simmering or warming oven for an hour or so, but the celery will continue to cook and soften

Freeze:

Yes. Beware of soggy celery as it reheats!

1 Separate the celery stalks and trim, removing the stringy outer bits from the bigger stalks. Cut into 4" (10cms) chunks.

2 Peel and chop the onion, crush the garlic and slice the carrots.

3 Heat the oil in a pan on the boiling plate and add all the ingredients. Cover with a tight fitting lid and when the lid is too hot to leave your hand on comfortably, move the pan to the simmering oven to cook for about 15 minutes.

4 Serve the celery with some bread to mop up the juices.

Alternative:

• Use trimmed fennel instead of the celery

beetroot toad
in the hole

Makes 4 individual servings

2 large beetroot

2 eggs

4 oz (110g) plain flour

½ pint (300 ml) milk

Pinch of salt

2 tbsp rapeseed oil

Oven:

Roasting oven, 220C, 450F, Gas 7

Prepare in advance:

Cooked, cooled toads will keep in the fridge for 24 hours

Prepare ahead:

Remove cooked toads from the oven, leave to cool and then reheat for 5 minutes before serving

Freeze:

Yes, reheat from frozen in the roasting oven for about 8 minutes

1   If using raw beetroot, put them, whole, into the roasting oven for about half an hour to cook. Remove from the oven and allow to cool before peeling them, then cut into rough chunks.

2   Meanwhile, put the plain shelf into the roasting oven on the 3rd runners.

3   Put a little oil into each hole of a 4–hole Yorkshire pudding tin and divide the beetroot chunks between the holes. Set the tin on top of the plain shelf in the oven.

4   Put the eggs, salt and flour into a wide jug and mix to a paste. Add the milk a little at a time, whisking until it is all incorporated.

5   Pour the batter into the hot tin and bake on top of the heated shelf for 15 – 20 minutes.

6   Serve at once.

Alternatives:

- Use chunks of roasted butternut squash instead of the beetroot
- Use raw mushrooms instead of the beetroot

Aga tip: Putting the plain shelf into the oven before cooking the batter traps the heat above the shelf and raises the temperature for really puffy toads

cheese and vegetable pie

To feed more people: Double the ingredients will fill the large roasting tin and should serve up to 10

Serves 4 – 5

Topping:

2 lb (900g) potatoes

¼ pint (150ml) milk

1 oz (25g) butter

Salt and pepper

2 oz (55g) cheddar cheese

Filling:

1 lb (450g) leeks

1 lb (450g) broccoli

8 oz (225g) peas

1 tub (200g) cream cheese

2 tbsp grainy mustard

2 oz (55g) cheddar cheese

Oven:

Simmering oven, 130C, 250F, Gas 1 and roasting oven, 200C, 400F, Gas 6

Prepare in advance:

Prepared pie will keep in the fridge for 24 hours

Prepare ahead:

Cooked pie will keep warm in the simmering or warming oven for an hour

Freeze:

Yes

1 Set the tub of cream cheese and the milk and butter onto the back of the Aga to warm up. Grate the cheddar.

2 Cut the potatoes into even sized chunks and put into a pan of cold water. Set on the boiling plate and bring to a fierce boil. Drain the water from the pan, cover with a lid and put into the simmering oven for about 25 minutes until the potatoes are soft.

3 Slice the leeks and cut the broccoli into florets.

4 Put the leeks, peas and broccoli into a pan, cover with cold water and a lid. Set the pan onto the boiling plate and when it is boiling really hard, drain the vegetables. Tip them into a bowl of very cold water. Drain and tip into fresh cold water, then drain again.

5 Tip the warm cream cheese, mustard and 2oz of cheddar into the pan with the vegetables and stir in.

6 When the potatoes are soft, take them from the simmering oven and mash with the warm milk and butter.

7 Pile the creamy vegetables into an oven proof dish or small roasting tin and spread with the mashed potatoes. Scatter over the remaining grated cheese and bake for about half an hour on the second runners in the roasting oven until the cheese is melted and golden.

Aga tip: Draining the vegetables and tipping them into two changes of very cold water stops them from cooking and sets the bright green colour

stir-fried shredded potatoes

Serves 4

1lb (450g) potatoes, thinly sliced

salt and freshly ground black pepper

1 tbsp groundnut oil

2 cloves garlic

2 tbsp fresh ginger

2 tbsp pickled ginger

2 red chillies

2 tbsp sugar

2 tbsp Shaoxing rice wine (or dry sherry)

2 tsp chilli oil

1½ tsp roasted and ground Sichuan peppercorns

Oven:

Boiling plate

Prepare ahead:

Not really, this is a cook and go dish

Freeze:

No

1 Stack the potato slices and cut them into matchsticks. Soak them in a bowl of cold water with a teaspoon of salt for five minutes, then drain thoroughly and blot them dry on a tea towel.

2 Chop the garlic, fresh ginger, chillies and pickled ginger.

3 Put a heavy sauté pan or casserole or large frying pan into the roasting oven to heat up.

4 Move the pan to the boiling plate and add the oil, and when it is hot, add the garlic, the fresh and pickled gingers and the chillies and stir-fry for about 30 seconds.

5 Season with salt and pepper, then add the potatoes and gently stir-fry for a couple of minutes until they are well coated with the spices and flavourings.

6 Add the sugar and rice wine (or sherry) and continue to stir-fry gently over a high heat for five minutes, or until most of the water has evaporated and the potatoes are cooked.

7 At this point, add the chilli oil, sprinkle on the peppercorns and serve at once.

spinach risotto

To feed more people: Double the ingredients will feed up to 9

Serves 4

8 oz (½ pint/300ml in a measuring jug) risotto rice

1 pint (550ml) vegetable stock

1 onion

1 clove garlic

½ lb (225g) spinach

2 tbsp rapeseed oil

3 oz (85g) blue cheese

Oven:

Simmering oven, 130C, 250F, Gas 1

Prepare in advance:

Will keep in the fridge for up to 24 hours

Prepare ahead:

Will keep warm in the simmering or warming oven for an extra hour or two

Freeze:

Yes

1　Peel and chop the onion, crush the garlic.

2　Heat the oil in a large casserole and add the onions and garlic. Cover and when the lid of the pan is too hot to rest your hand on, transfer the pan to the simmering oven for about 15 minutes for the onions to soften.

3　Move the pan to the simmering plate and add the risotto rice and stock. Cover, bring to the boil and return the pan to the simmering oven for about half an hour, until all the stock has been absorbed.

4　Take the risotto out of the oven, add the spinach and cheese and leave to stand for 5 minutes while the cheese melts and the spinach wilts. Stir and serve.

dudhi daal

This is a lovely vegetarian main course, or it makes a delicious accompaniment to a curry or grilled chicken!

To feed more people: This will serve up to 8 as part of a larger curry meal, or double the quantity will go around up to 15.

Serves 4

4 oz (110g) red lentils

4 oz (110g) split peas

1 large onion

1 dudhi or 2 courgettes or a small butternut squash or pumpkin

2 cloves garlic

2 tbsp sunflower oil

1 pint (550ml) stock

1" / 2cms piece fresh ginger

2 tsp garam masala

1 tsp smoked paprika

½ tsp salt

4 oz (110g) cherry tomatoes

1 tbsp chopped fresh coriander

Oven:

Simmering oven, 130C, 250F, Gas 1

Prepare in advance:

Cooked, cooled daal will keep in the fridge for up to 48 hours: the flavour improving as it matures

Prepare ahead:

Will keep warm in simmering oven for up to an hour

Freeze:

No, the vegetables go rubbery as they defrost

1   Peel and chop the onion, crush the garlic and peel and chop the ginger. Chop the dudhi into ½"/1cm cubes.

2   Heat the oil in a heavy pan and add the onion, dudhi, garlic and ginger. Stir over the heat and, once sizzling, cover and transfer to the simmering oven for about 10 minutes to soften.

3   Take the pan of onions from the oven, transfer to the simmering plate and stir in the garam masala, paprika and salt. Fry briefly to release the flavours, then add the lentils and stock. Bring to the boil then cover and put into the simmering oven for about 15 – 20 minutes.

4   Cut the tomatoes into halves and chop the coriander. When the lentils are cooked, stir in the tomatoes and coriander and serve.

Alternatives:

• Use 2 courgettes instead of the dudhi

• Use a small butternut squash instead of the dudhi

• Use a small pumpkin instead of the dudhi

spinach and
mushroom lasagne

To feed more people: Double the ingredients will fill the large roasting tin and should serve up to 10

Serves 4

6 sheets no-cook lasagne

2 x tubs (2 x 200g) ricotta cheese

1 lb (450g) mushrooms

3 large onions

2 cloves garlic

2 lb (900g) spinach

1 tbsp rapeseed oil

1 tbsp butter

Salt and pepper

Fresh nutmeg

1 quantity heart attack sauce
(p. 178)

Oven:

Simmering oven, 130C, 250F, Gas 1 and roasting oven, 200C, 400F, Gas 6

Prepare in advance:

Assembled lasagne will keep in the fridge for 24 hours

Prepare ahead:

Will keep warm in the simmering or warming oven for an hour

Freeze:

Yes, assembled and not baked

If you do not want to cook a full scale lasagne, mix the spinach and mushrooms with some cooked pasta and pour the cream sauce over

1   Set the ricotta onto the back of the Aga to warm up and soften.

2   Peel and chop the onions. Wipe and chop the mushrooms. Peel and crush the garlic.

3   Heat the oil and butter in a large sauté pan on the boiling plate and add the onions, garlic and mushrooms. Put the lid onto the pan and when the lid is too hot to leave your hand on comfortably, transfer the pan to the simmering oven for about 20 minutes.

4   Move the pan of cooked onions, garlic and mushrooms to the boiling plate and remove the lid. Add the spinach and replace the lid. (You may have to wait for some of the spinach to wilt before it will all fit into the pan!)

5   Put the pan onto the floor of the roasting oven for 5 minutes until the spinach has wilted, then take off the lid and leave the pan on the floor of the oven for another 5 minutes or so to boil off some of the liquid. Season with salt, pepper and grated nutmeg and stir in the softened ricotta.

6   Put a third of the spinach mixture into the deep Portmeirion roasting dish or the small roasting tin, and lay three sheets of lasagne over it. Continue with a second layer of spinach, the remaining lasagne sheets and then the rest of the spinach.

7   Pour the prepared heart attack sauce over the lasagne and slide the tin onto the second runners in the roasting oven for about 15 minutes until the sauce is bubbling and golden.

Alternative:
Use white sauce instead of the rich cream and rosemary sauce, or just some seasoned crème fraîche, maybe topped with a little grated cheese for a lower fat version!

roasted broccoli with
chickpeas

To feed more people: Double the ingredients will feed up to 10

Serves 4

2 heads broccoli (about 1½lb, 650g)

2 cloves garlic

2 tsp cumin seeds

2 tsp coriander seeds

2 tbsp rapeseed oil

1 tin (400g) chickpeas

1 pack (100g) pine nuts

Oven:

Roasting oven, 200C, 400F, Gas 6

Prepare in advance:

Cut up the broccoli up to 12 hours ahead

Prepare ahead:

Will keep warm in the warming or simmering oven for half an hour

Freeze:

No

1 Cut the broccoli into small florets. Crush the garlic and open and drain the can of chickpeas.

2 Line the large shallow baking tray with Bake-O-Glide.

3 Put the broccoli, garlic, seeds and oil into the tin and shake to mix.

4 Hang the tin from the 2nd runners in the roasting oven and roast for about 25 minutes.

5 Add the chickpeas and pine nuts to the tin, shake to mix and return to the 2nd runners in the roasting oven for a further 10 minutes until warmed through.

6 Serve warm, or cooled as a salad with a French dressing poured over.

cheesy potato puffs

To feed more people: If you are less generous when filling the muffin cups, this will divide into 8. Double the quantity will fill 12–14 muffin cups if you have a second muffin tin!

Serves 6

1 oz (25g) butter

1 lb (450g) potatoes

4 spring onions

2 oz (55g) grated cheddar cheese

3 tbsp milk

2 eggs

Nutmeg

Salt and pepper

Oven:

Simmering oven, 130C, 250F, Gas 1 and roasting oven, 200C, 400F, Gas 6

Prepare in advance:

Unbaked potato puffs will keep – in the muffin tin – in the fridge for up to 24 hours

Prepare ahead:

Will keep warm in the simmering or warming oven for an hour or so

Freeze:

Unbaked potato puffs – in the muffin tin. Bake from frozen for 25 minutes

1 Set the butter in a bowl on the back of the Aga to melt. Put the milk in a mug on the back of the Aga to warm up.

2 Cut the potatoes into chunks and put into a pan just big enough to hold them. Cover with water, put on the lid and bring to the boil on the boiling plate. When the pan is boiling hard, drain off all the water, replace the lid and put the pan into the simmering oven for about half an hour until the potatoes are soft.

3 Brush a non-stick six-hole muffin tin with the melted butter.

4 Trim and slice the spring onions and put them into a bowl with the cheese, warm milk, leftover butter and cooked potatoes – mash everything together. Season well with salt and pepper and a few grates of nutmeg.

5 Separate the eggs and beat the yolks into the potato mixture. Whisk the whites and fold them in as well.

6 Divide the mixture between the muffin cups.

7 Set the grid shelf on the 4th, lowest runners in the roasting oven and put the muffin tin onto it. Bake for about 15 minutes until puffed up and golden brown.

tortilla, *spanish omelette*

6–7 medium potatoes, peeled

1 onion

5–6 large eggs

¼ pint (150ml) olive oil

Salt to taste

Oven:

Simmering oven, 130C, 250F, Gas 1, then roasting oven, 200C, 400F, Gas 6

Prepare in advance:

Cook the potatoes and onions up to 24 hours in advance, but cook the eggs just before serving

Prepare ahead:

Will keep warm in the simmering or warming oven for half an hour

Freeze:

No, the eggs go rubbery

1 Cut the potatoes in half lengthwise. Then, with the flat side on the cutting surface, slice the potato approximately 1/8" thick.

2 Peel and chop the onion. Put the potatoes and onions into a bowl and mix them together.

3 Heat the olive oil in a large sauté pan. Tip potato and onion mixture into the pan. Cover with a tight fitting lid. Set the pan onto the simmering plate and when the lid is too hot to leave your hand on, move the pan to the simmering oven for about half an hour until the potatoes are soft.

4 Break the eggs into a bowl, season well and whisk. Pour into the cooked potatoes and stir about. Set the pan onto the simmering plate.

5 Allow the egg to cook for about 5 minutes, then carefully lift up one side of the omelette to check if the egg has slightly browned. The inside of the mixture should not be completely cooked and the egg will still be runny.

6 While the egg is cooking, slide the grid shelf onto the second runners in the roasting oven.

7 When the mixture has browned on the bottom, slide the pan onto the grid shelf and cook the top of the omelette for about 3–4 minutes. Remove from the oven and let the tortilla sit in the pan for 2 minutes before sliding onto a plate to serve, hot, tepid or cold, possibly with tomato sauce.

fig and blue cheese tart

To feed more people: Double the ingredients will fill a 12"/30cms dish and should cut into at least 10 slices

Serves 4

For the pastry:

6 oz (175g) plain flour

3 oz (85g) butter

1 tbsp Parmesan cheese

2–3 tbsp water

1 tsp poppy seeds

½ tsp mixed dried herbs

Up to 3 tbsp water

For the filling:

2 onions

1 tbsp rapeseed oil

3 eggs

½ pint (300ml) crème fraîche

Salt and pepper

4 figs

5 oz (150g) Roquefort or other soft blue cheese

Oven:

Simmering oven, 130C, 250F, Gas 1 and floor of roasting oven

Prepare in advance:

Cooked, cooled onions will keep in the fridge for 24 hours, as will the raw pastry case

Prepare ahead:

Will keep warm in the simmering or warming oven for half an hour

Freeze:

Yes, but it may be a little watery when it defrosts. Easier to freeze the uncooked pastry case and use straight from the freezer

1   To make the pastry, put the flour, butter, poppy seeds, herbs and Parmesan into a processor and whizz until the texture of breadcrumbs. With the motor running, add the water a spoonful at a time until it comes together as a dough.

2   Roll out the pastry and line a 9"/23cm flan dish. Chill or freeze until required.

3   Peel and slice the onions.

4   Heat the oil in a pan on the boiling plate and add the onions. Put the lid on the pan and when the lid is too hot to rest your hand on, there will be enough steam in the pan that the onions are at boiling point. Put the pan into the simmering oven for 15 minutes until they are soft.

5   Mix together the crème fraîche, eggs and seasoning. Add this to the onion mixture then pour into the pastry case.

6   Halve the figs and arrange on top of the onions in the pastry. Cut the cheese into small lumps and scatter these over the top of the tart.

7   Put the dish onto the floor of the roasting oven and bake for about 25 minutes until the cheese has melted and puffed up a bit.

cauliflower with onions

To feed more people: This will feed up to 6 as part of a curry buffet. For vegetarians, it will serve 2–3. Double the quantity will serve up to 6, or 8 if an accompaniment to a meat dish

Serves 4

1 cauliflower

1 tbsp rapeseed oil

3 onions

1 tbsp sundried tomato purée

1 tsp caster sugar

1 tbsp red wine vinegar

1 tbsp fresh thyme leaves

2 oz (55g) pine nuts

2 oz (55g) raisins

Salt and pepper

Oven:

Simmering oven, 130C, 250F, Gas 1

Prepare in advance:

Will keep in the fridge for up to 24 hours

Prepare ahead:

Will keep warm in the simmering or warming oven for an hour

Freeze:

Yes, but the cauliflower will be very soft when reheated

1   Peel and slice the onions. Trim the cauliflower and divide it into florets.

2   Heat the oil in a heavy pan and add the onions. Cover with a lid and heat the pan until the lid is too hot to touch easily – there will be enough steam in the pan to cook the onions.

3   Move the pan of onions to the simmering oven for up to half an hour to soften and colour slightly.

4   When the onions are soft, move the pan to the simmering plate and add the tomato purée, vinegar, sugar and thyme. Season well and cook for a minute or two.

5   Add the cauliflower and about ¼ pint (150ml) water to the pan. Bring to the boil then cover and return it to the simmering oven for 10 minutes, until the cauliflower is just tender.

6   Once the cauliflower is cooked, add the raisins and pine nuts, and serve with a scattering of chopped parsley to show you have made an effort, or possibly some cherry tomatoes for a bit of colour.

cauliflower and
potato curry

To feed more people: Double the ingredients will feed up to 10, especially if served as part of a curry buffet

Optional extra: Add some chopped green chillies with the garlic if you like a kick

Serves 4

   1 medium cauliflower

   3 Maris Piper potatoes

   1 onion

   2 cloves garlic

   1 tbsp rapeseed oil

   1 tsp cumin seeds

   ½ tsp mustard seeds

   1 tsp smoked paprika

   ¼ tsp salt

   1 tbsp sun dried tomato purée

   3 tbsp water

Oven:

   Simmering oven, 130C, 250F, Gas 1

Prepare in advance:

   Cooked, cooled curry will keep in the fridge for 24 hours

Prepare ahead:

   Will keep warm for an hour or so in the simmering or warming oven – tip the lid of the pan slightly so that the steam escapes and the cauliflower stops cooking

Freeze:

   Yes, but the cauliflower will be very soft when reheated

1   Peel and chop the onion, crush the garlic. Cut the potatoes into ½", 1cm cubes. Cut the cauliflower into small florets.

2   Heat the oil in a sauté pan on the boiling plate and add the onions and potatoes. Cover at once and when the lid of the pan is too hot to leave your hand on comfortably, transfer the pan to the simmering oven for 20 minutes to soften the vegetables.

3   Move the pan of softened potato and onion to the simmering plate and stir in the garlic, spices and salt. Stir around on the heat for a minute then add the cauliflower, water and tomato puree. When boiling, cover and put the pan back into the simmering oven for 15 minutes to cook the cauliflower.

4   Serve with some chopped parsley scattered over the top to show you have made an effort.

braised mushrooms

To feed more people: Double the ingredients will serve up to 9, three packs of mushrooms with double the sauce will feed 14 as an accompaniment to another main dish

Serves 3 – 4

2 x packs whole dried mushrooms

2 tbsp caster sugar

2 tbsp dark soy sauce

1 tbsp rapeseed oil

1 tbsp sesame oil

½ tsp salt

4 cloves garlic

1" (2.5cms) piece fresh ginger

1 tbsp oyster sauce

Oven:

Simmering oven, 130C, 250F, Gas 1

Prepare in advance:

Will keep in the fridge for several days, but serve at room temperature

Freeze:

No

1   Put the mushrooms into a pan and pour over a pint of boiling water. Leave to stand for half an hour.

2   Crush the garlic and chop the ginger very finely.

3   Bring the pan to the boil and add the rest of the ingredients, except the oyster sauce. Cover and put into the simmering oven for about 45 minutes until the mushrooms are tender.

4   Remove the pan from the oven and leave to cool until tepid. Stir in the oyster sauce and serve.

butternut squash risotto

To feed more people: Double the ingredients will feed up to 9

Serves 4

8 oz (½ pint/300ml in a measuring jug) risotto rice

1 pint (550ml) vegetable stock

1 onion

1 clove garlic

1 medium butternut squash

2 tbsp rapeseed oil

3 oz (85g) gorgonzola

Oven:

Simmering oven, 130C, 250F, Gas 1

Prepare in advance:

Will keep in the fridge for up to 24 hours

Prepare ahead:

Will keep warm in the simmering or warming oven for an extra hour or two

Freeze:

Yes.

1   Put the squash, whole, into the roasting oven for half an hour. Remove from the oven and allow to cool.

2   Peel and chop the onion, crush the garlic.

3   Heat the oil in a large casserole and add the onions and garlic. Cover and when the lid of the pan is too hot to rest your hand on, transfer the pan to the simmering oven for about 15 minutes for the onions to soften.

4   Peel and chop the squash, discarding the seeds.

5   Move the pan to the simmering plate and add the risotto rice, squash and stock. Cover, bring to the boil and return the pan to the simmering oven for about half an hour, until all the stock has been absorbed.

6   Take the risotto out of the oven, add the cheese and leave to stand for 5 minutes while the cheese melts. Stir and serve with a scattering of chopped parsley.

roasted spiced carrots

Serves 4 – 5

1lb (450g) carrots

2 tbsp sunflower oil

1 tbsp smoked paprika

Oven:

Roasting oven, 200C, 400F, Gas 6

Prepare ahead:

Allow to cool then reheat in
roasting oven for about 5 minutes

Freeze:

*Yes, reheat for about 8 minutes in
roasting oven*

1 Line the small shallow baking tray with Bake-O-Glide.

2 Cut the carrots in half lengthways and remove the tops.

3 Pile into the roasting tin with the oil and smoked paprika. Shake well to coat with the oil.

4 Hang the tin from the second set of runners and roast for about 15 minutes, season and serve.

Aga tip: Roast all vegetables in a shallow tin, rather than a deep roasting tin, so that the heat from all sides of the oven can crisp them up

broccoli and mushrooms with ginger and chilli

Serves 4

6 oz (175g) mushrooms

6 oz (175g) broccoli

2 tbsp rapeseed oil

1"/2½ cm piece root ginger

1 clove garlic

1 small red chilli

1 tsp sun dried tomato purée

1 tbsp dark soy sauce

1 tbsp rice vinegar

1 tsp sesame oil

Oven:

Roasting oven to heat the pan, then boiling plate

Prepare in advance:

Chop all the ingredients and keep in the fridge for up to 12 hours before cooking

Prepare ahead:

No, this is a cook and go meal!

Freeze:

No

1   Put a large, wide based heavy sauté pan into the roasting oven to heat up before you start preparing the vegetables.

2   Quarter the mushrooms and cut the broccoli into florets the same size as the mushroom quarters. Peel and chop the ginger and garlic. Halve the chilli and remove the seeds, then chop finely. Mix together the garlic, ginger and chilli.

3   Mix together the tomato purée, soy sauce, rice vinegar and sesame oil (in a jam jar is easiest).

4   Transfer the hot pan to the boiling plate and heat the oil in it.

5   Tip the mushrooms and broccoli into the hot pan and stir fry for a couple of minutes.

6   Tip the garlic and onion mixture into the pan and stir fry for a further minute, then pour in the soy sauce mixture and stir until boiling.

7   Serve at once.

beetroot risotto

To feed more people: Double the ingredients will feed up to 9

Serves 4

8 oz (½ pint/300ml in a measuring jug) risotto rice

1 pint (550ml) vegetable stock

1 onion

1 clove garlic

2 large beetroot

2 tbsp rapeseed oil

3 oz (85g) goats' cheese

Oven:

Simmering oven, 130C, 250F, Gas 1

Prepare in advance:

Will keep in the fridge for up to 24 hours

Prepare ahead:

Will keep warm in the simmering or warming oven for an extra hour or two

Freeze:

Yes

1 If using raw, fresh beetroot, put them, whole, into the roasting oven for half an hour. Remove from the oven, trim the leaves off and allow to cool.

2 Peel and chop the onion, crush the garlic.

3 Heat the oil in a large casserole and add the onions and garlic. Cover and when the lid of the pan is too hot to rest your hand on, transfer the pan to the simmering oven for about 15 minutes for the onions to soften.

4 Grate the beetroot – use a processor or put rubber gloves on, or you will have purple hands for a week.

5 Move the pan to the simmering plate and add the risotto rice, grated beetroot and stock. Cover, bring to the boil and return the pan to the simmering oven for about half an hour, until all the stock has been absorbed.

6 Take the risotto out of the oven, add the cheese and leave to stand for 5 minutes while the cheese melts. Stir and serve with a scattering of chopped parsley.

salmon roulade with smoked salmon

Serves 6 – 10, depending upon how thick the slices are!

5oz (150g) salmon fillet

4 eggs

Salt and pepper

Filling:

1 tbsp dill sauce

8 oz (225g) cream cheese

4 oz (110g) smoked salmon slices

Oven:

Baking oven, 180C, 350F, Gas 4

Prepare in advance:

Will keep in the fridge for up to 24 hours

Freeze:

Yes, wrap the finished roulade in kitchen paper and a plastic bag to freeze – defrost rolled in the kitchen paper to absorb any moisture that comes off the roulade as it warms up

1　Line the large roasting tin with Bake-O-Glide.

2　Separate eggs and whizz the yolks, salmon and seasoning to a paste. Beat the white until stiff then fold into the mixture.

3　Spread over the tin and bake for about 10 minutes.

4　2 oven Aga: Hang the roasting tin from the 4th, lowest runners in the roasting oven with the cold plan shelf on the 2nd runners above.

5　3, 4 and 5 oven Aga: Hang the tin from the 3rd runners in the baking oven.

6　When the roulade is cooked, turn it out onto a clean tea towel, remove paper, roll in the tea towel and leave to cool.

7　Beat the cream cheese with the dill and seasoning. Unroll the roulade and spread with the cheese filling. Lay on the slices of smoked salmon then roll up tightly and chill until set.

8　To serve, cut into 1″/2cm slices and arrange on a plate, decorated with sprigs of dill or parsley.

Aga tip: Roll the roulade along its short side to make a short, fat, roll if you know how many people you are feeding. Roll it along its long side to make a longer, thinner roll if you think you may need to stretch it around more people

fish and bean bake

To feed more people: Double the ingredients and 10 pieces of fish will fill the large roasting tin – cover with foil to contain the steam as it cooks

Serves 4

4 large white fish steaks

1 onion

1 clove garlic

1 chorizo sausage piece (about 8 oz / 225g)

1 tin (400g) haricot beans

1 tin (400g) butter beans

1 tin (400g) chopped tomatoes

1 tbsp sundried tomato purée

Oven:

Floor of roasting oven

Prepare in advance:

Cooked, cooled sauce will keep in the fridge for 24 hours, add the raw fish and reheat in the roasting oven for 20 minutes

Prepare ahead:

Will keep warm in the simmering or warming oven for half an hour

Freeze:

Cooked, cooled sauce and raw fish. Defrost then bake for 30 minutes in roasting oven

1   Peel and chop the onion and garlic. Cut the chorizo into slices. Open the tins of beans and drain them.

2   Put the onion, garlic and chorizo into a sauté pan and set it on the floor of the roasting oven for about 10 minutes. The chorizo will give off enough oil to fry the onions.

3   Move the pan to the boiling plate and add the beans, tomatoes and tomato purée. Bring to the boil then lay in the pieces of fish. Cover with a lid and put the pan back into the roasting oven for 5 – 8 minutes until the fish is cooked.

4   Serve with a green vegetable and some bread to mop up the sauce.

rosti fish pie

To feed more people: Double the ingredients will fill the large roasting tin and should feed 10

Serves 4

For the topping:

1 lb (450g) new or waxy potatoes

2 oz (55g) butter

Salt and pepper

For the base:

1½ lb (700g) white fish, skinned and boned

1 tub (200g) cream cheese

1 tbsp Dijon mustard

Oven:

Simmering oven 130C, 250F, Gas 1 and roasting oven, 200C, 400F, Gas 6

Prepare in advance:

Assembled, unbaked pie will keep in the fridge for 24 hours

Prepare ahead:

Will keep warm in the simmering or warming oven for an hour

Freeze:

Assembled, uncooked pie

1 Put the potatoes into a pan, cover with cold water and bring to the boil. When boiling hard, drain off all the water, cover with a lid and put the pan into the simmering oven for about 25 minutes for the potatoes to soften.

2 Set the butter in a big bowl on the back of the Aga to melt. Set the tub of cream cheese onto the back of the Aga to warm up and soften.

3 Take the cooked potatoes from the oven and grate coarsely – easiest in a processor. Toss the potatoes with the melted butter and season well.

4 Cut the fish into 1"/2½ cms pieces and tip into a bowl. Add the cream cheese and mustard and mix together. Season well.

5 Tip the fish into an ovenproof dish and pile the potatoes on top.

6 Slide the grid shelf onto the 3rd runners in the roasting oven and put the dish onto it.

7 Bake for about 25 minutes until crispy and golden on top and the sauce is bubbling below.

Freezing tip: Assemble the pie in a dish lined with cling film. Cover the top with more cling film and freeze. When frozen, tip out of the dish, wrap in a plastic bag, label and freeze. When ready to eat the pie, take from the freezer, unwrap and put back into the dish, which it fits perfectly! Defrost and bake.

smoked haddock tart

Serves 4

1 pack ready rolled puff pastry

1 lb (450g) smoked haddock

1 tub (400g) mascarpone

2 tbsp horseradish sauce

1 egg

2 oz (55g) grated Cheddar

1 tbsp chopped fresh parsley to finish

Oven:

Roasting oven, 400F, 200C, Gas 6

Prepare in advance:

Assemble the tart and keep in the fridge for up to 6 hours before baking, but it really is nicest eaten on the day it is baked

Prepare ahead:

Will keep warm in the simmering oven for half an hour

Freeze:

Yes

1 Set the tub of mascarpone onto to the back of the Aga to warm up and soften.

2 Cut the fish into ½"/1cm chunks.

3 Unroll the pastry onto a piece of Bake-O-Glide laid on the cold plain shelf.

4 Beat the egg with a fork and brush the outer inch (2cm) of the pastry with the egg, then tip the contents of the tub of mascarpone into the egg bowl, add the horseradish and fish and mix together.

5 Spread the fish and mascarpone mix over the pastry, leaving the border free. Scatter the cheese over the top of the mascarpone mix.

6 Slide the tart, on its Bake-O-Glide, off the plain shelf and onto the floor of the roasting oven and bake for about 15 minutes until the pastry is puffed and golden.

7 To remove from the oven, slide the plain shelf under the Bake-O-Glide and pull onto the shelf.

8 Serve warm or cold, with a scattering of chopped parsley.

prawn and chorizo rice
– not quite paella!

To feed more people: Double the ingredients will stretch around 9, add extra rice and stock to the same amount of other ingredients for a more filling meal

Serves 4

1 tbsp rapeseed oil

1 onion

1 green pepper

4 oz (110g) small chorizo sausages

2 cloves garlic

1 green chilli

8 oz (225g) long grain rice

¾ pint (450ml) stock

8 oz (225g) raw prawns

4 oz (110g) frozen petits pois

1 lemon

Oven:

Floor of roasting oven, simmering oven 130C, 250F, Gas 1

Prepare ahead:

The pan of cooked rice will sit in the simmering or warming oven for an extra hour or two, but wait to add the prawns and peas until 5 minutes before serving

Freeze:

Yes, but be sure to cool the rice as fast as you can and reheat in the roasting oven for 20 minutes

1   Peel and chop the onion, crush the garlic, chop the pepper, chop the chilli and cut the chorizo sausages into ½" chunks.

2   Heat the oil in a heavy sauté pan and add the onion, peppers, chorizo, chilli and garlic. Set the pan onto the floor of the roasting oven to fry for about 5 minutes, then return to the boiling plate and add the rice and stock.

3   Bring to the boil, then cover and transfer to the simmering oven for 15 minutes.

4   Move the pan back to the boiling plate and add the prawns and peas. Stir and leave to stand for 5 minutes to cook the prawns and defrost the peas.

5   Serve with a squeeze of lemon juice.

galician fish

To feed more people: Double the quantity will stretch around 9, especially if you cut the fish into small-ish pieces

Serves 4

2 large hake or fresh cod steaks

3 or 4 potatoes

1 onion

4 cloves garlic crushed

fresh parsley

salt

½ tsp thyme

1 bay leaf

8 tbsp rapeseed oil

5 tbsp white wine

½ tsp paprika

Oven:

Aga simmering oven, 130C, 250F, Gas 1

Prepare in advance:

Cooked, cooled potato base will keep in the fridge for 24 hours, warm through in simmering oven for half an hour then add the raw fish and continue

Prepare ahead:

Potato base will keep warm in the simmering or warming oven for up to an hour

Freeze:

Don't see why not

1 Slice the potatoes and chop the onion, peel and crush one clove of the garlic. Peel and slice the rest of the garlic.

2 Place the potato slices, chopped onion, 1 clove of crushed garlic, bay leaf, fresh parsley, thyme and a couple of pinches of salt in a casserole dish – sprinkle with 1 tbsp rapeseed oil and 4 tbsp of the wine.

3 Add water to just cover everything in the pan and bring to the boil. Cover and transfer to the simmering oven for 20 minutes until the potatoes are soft.

4 Remove the pan from the oven and place the fish steaks on top of the potatoes. Replace the lid on the pan and put back into the simmering oven for a further 10 minutes.

5 Heat the remaining rapeseed oil in a frying pan and add the garlic slices and sauté for a couple of minutes, then add the paprika and 1 tbsp wine. Shake over the heat and pour over the fish to serve.

fennel and monkfish salad

Serves 4

1½ lb (600g) monkfish tail

3 tbsp white wine

Salt and pepper

1 bulb fennel

3 tbsp mayonnaise

2 tbsp cream

Fennel leaves to garnish

Oven:

Roasting oven, 180C, 350F, Gas 4

Prepare in advance:

Will keep in the fridge for up to 24 hours

Freeze:

No

1 Skin the fish and place in the small roasting tin. Pour over the wine, season and cover with foil.

2 Hang the tin from the 3rd runners in the roasting oven and bake for 15 minutes until the fish is opaque, then remove from the oven and allow to cool. When cool, cut into chunks.

3 Wash the fennel bulb and slice it finely.

4 Mix the mayonnaise and cream, season and toss in the fish and fennel.

5 Serve, garnished with fennel leaves, with green salad.

smoky fishcakes

To feed more people: Make 10 or even 12 smaller fishcakes from this mixture, each wrapped in a rasher of bacon, or double the quantity will make 16 – 20 fishcakes

Makes 8

1½ lb (600g) King Edward potatoes

1 lb (450g) smoked cod

1 egg

1 pack (200g) cream cheese

2 oz (55g) Cheddar cheese

Salt and pepper

8 rashers streaky bacon

Oven:

Simmering oven, 130C, 250F, Gas 1 and roasting oven, 200C, 400F, Gas 6 or a grill

Prepare in advance:

Prepared fishcakes will keep in the fridge for 24 hours

Prepare ahead:

Cooked fishcakes will keep warm in the simmering or warming oven for half an hour

Freeze:

Yes, uncooked cakes

1 Cut the potatoes into even sized chunks and put into a pan, cover with cold water and set the pan onto the boiling plate, with the lid on. When the pan is boiling hard, drain off all the water and put it into the simmering oven for about half an hour, until the potatoes are soft.

2 Meanwhile, line a small shallow baking tray with Bake-O-Glide and set the fish into it. Hang the tin from the third runners in the roasting oven and cook for about 10 minutes until the fish flakes easily.

3 Set the pack of cream cheese onto the back of the Aga to soften and grate the cheddar.

4 Take the cooked fish from the oven and tip it into a bowl and break up with a fork.

5 When the potatoes are soft, mash them with the softened cream cheese, egg and cheddar. Season well, then mix into the cooked fish. Set aside to cool.

6 Divide the fish mixture into 8 and shape each portion into a fishcake. Wrap a rasher of bacon around each fishcake.

7 Put the fishcakes into the tin that you used for cooking the fish, hang it from the second runners in the roasting oven and cook for about ten minutes until the bacon is golden and crispy.

Alternative: use leftover fish pie and shape into fishcakes, wrap in bacon and grill against the top of the oven

steamed sea bream
with coriander sauce

Serves 4

1 x 1½lb (675g) whole, large sea
bream, cleaned

2 large pinches of five spice
powder

2 large pinches of sea salt

For the sauce:

1 garlic clove

1" / 2.5cm piece fresh root ginger

2 small red chillies

2 spring onions

Handful fresh basil

Large handful of fresh coriander

5–6 tbsp groundnut oil

¼ tsp sea salt

2–3 tbsp light soy sauce

Oven:

Roasting oven (or baking oven if
you want the fish to cook for half
an hour!) 180C, 350F, Gas 4

Prepare ahead:

Eat as soon as the fish is cooked

Freeze:

No

1   Season the fish with the five spice powder, then
season with salt on both sides.

2   Pour about ¼ pint / 150 ml water into the small
roasting tin. Lay the fish into the grill rack (making
sure the base doesn't touch the water), cover with foil
and hang the tin from the 3rd runners in the roasting
oven for 10–15 minutes until the flesh of the fish turns
opaque and flakes when poked.

3   While the fish is cooking, chop the herbs, garlic,
ginger and chillies and slice the spring onions, then
add the rest of the sauce ingredients and mix well.

4   To serve, lift the fish onto a large plate and pour the
sauce over the fish and accompany with rice and
vegetables.

smoked mackerel and potato salad

To feed more people: Double the ingredients will feed up to 9, or more if served as part of a summer buffet

Serves 4

1 lb (500g bag) small new
potatoes
Small red onion
1 head of red chicory
Bag (100g) mixed lettuce leaves
3 fillets (100g) smoked mackerel

Dressing:

3 tbsp rapeseed oil
1 tbsp red wine vinegar
Salt and pepper
1 tbsp horseradish sauce

1 tbsp chopped fresh parsley to
serve

Oven:

Simmering oven

Prepare in advance:

Cooked, cooled potatoes and
salad will keep in the fridge for up
to 24 hours, do not dress the
leaves until just before serving

Prepare ahead:

Potatoes will keep warm in simmering or warming
oven for an hour or so before assembling the salad

Freeze:

No

1 Put the potatoes into a pan and cover them with cold
   water. Put the pan onto the boiling plate until it is
   boiling hard.

2 When the potatoes are boiling, drain off all the water,
   cover with a tight fitting lid and transfer to the
   simmering oven for at least half an hour to soften.

3 Peel the onion and chop it finely. Tip into a bowl with
   the dressing ingredients and mix well.

4 Slice the chicory and flake the fish fillets.

5 When the potatoes are cooked, remove from the oven
   and slice them into the bowl of onion dressing. Mix
   together.

6 Arrange the salad leaves on a wide plate, scatter over
   the chicory and fish, then pour over the warm
   potatoes and the dressing.

7 Scatter the parsley over the salad and serve.

Ring the changes:

- Use a head of Chinese leaves, finely shredded instead of the salad leaves, it will not wilt
  in the heat of the potatoes

- Use hot-smoked trout fillets instead of the mackerel

- Use smoked eel instead of the mackerel

traditional paella

To feed more people: Double the ingredients will serve up to 14, with a lot of salad and garlic bread

Serves 8

¾ pint in a measuring jug (350g) paella rice

2 tbsp oil

1 x 3 lb (1.35 kg) chicken, jointed into 8 pieces or 8 chicken thighs

1 large onion

1 red pepper

4 oz (110g) chorizo sausage in a piece

2 cloves garlic

1½ pints (900ml) stock or water

1 tsp smoked paprika

½ tsp saffron strands

8 oz (225g) ripe tomatoes

Small bag (250g) frozen mixed seafood

2 oz (55g) peas

Salt and pepper

Oven:

Floor of roasting oven, simmering oven, 130C, 250F, Gas 1

Prepare ahead:

Will keep warm in the simmering or warming oven for up to an hour, leave out the seafood and peas until just before serving

Freeze:

Not once the seafood has been added, otherwise yes

1 Peel and chop the onion, chop the pepper and peel and crush the garlic. Cut the chorizo into ½" / 1 cm chunks. Quarter the tomatoes.

2 Put the seafood and peas onto the back of the Aga to thaw and warm up.

3 Heat the oil in a casserole and add the chicken pieces, onion, pepper, garlic and chorizo. Set the pan onto the floor of the roasting oven and fry until the chicken is browned, about 10 minutes, shaking the pan once or twice.

4 Add the rice to the pan, together with the paprika and saffron and the tomatoes. Bring to the boil, stirring, then cover the pan and put it into the simmering oven for about half an hour.

5 Take the pan of cooked rice and chicken from the oven, stir in the seafood and peas. Re-cover the pan and put it back into the simmering oven for a further five minutes then serve.

salmon, coconut and lime parcels

Makes 6

1 tbsp groundnut oil

½ tin (200g) coconut milk

6 x 170g (6oz) salmon fillets, skin on

2 limes

1 clove garlic

2 sticks lemongrass

1 red chilli

3 tbsp soy sauce

Aga rice, to serve

Oven:

Roasting oven, 180C, 350F, Gas 4

Prepare in advance:

Assemble the parcels and keep in the fridge for 6 hours before baking

Prepare ahead:

Will keep warm in the simmering or warming oven for half an hour

Freeze:

Don't see why not, uncooked. Defrost before baking

1   Cut out 6 rectangles of foil big enough to enclose the fish and brush one side of each with the oil.

2   Chop the lemongrass, garlic and chill together. Grate the rind and squeeze the juice from the limes. Tip into a jam jar and add the soy sauce and coconut milk. Shake to combine.

3   Put a salmon fillet in the middle of the oiled side of each piece of foil. Raise the edges to create a bowl, then divide the coconut liquid between each parcel. Scrunch the foil to make sealed parcels.

4   Put the parcels into the large roasting tin and slide it into the roasting oven on the 3rd runners and bake for 12–15 minutes.

5   Serve in the foil parcels with lime wedges and rice.

creamy, crunchy pesto salmon

To feed more people: A whole salmon side will feed up to 8, or more if cut into smaller pieces!

Serves 4

½ salmon side (500g)

½ packet (100g) cream cheese

2 tbsp pesto

2 tbsp porridge oats

Oven:

Roasting oven, 200C, 400F, Gas 6

Prepare in advance:

Coat the fish, cover and keep in the fridge for 24 hours before cooking

Prepare ahead:

Will keep warm in the simmering or warming oven for half an hour

Freeze:

Yes, raw, coated fish

1 Set the cream cheese onto the back of the Aga to warm up and soften.

2 Line a shallow baking tray with Bake-O-Glide.

3 Lay the fish into the prepared tray, skin side down.

4 Stir the pesto into the cream cheese and spread this over the fish. Scatter the oats on top of the cream cheese mixture.

5 Hang the tin on the 2nd runners in the roasting oven and bake for about 15 minutes, or in the baking oven for half an hour.

6 Serve!

chilli and celeriac fish pie

To feed more people: Double the ingredients will fill the large roasting tin and may feed up to 12

Serves 4 – 5

¾ lb (375g) potatoes

¾ lb (375g) celeriac

¼ pint milk

1 oz butter

Salt and pepper

1½ lb haddock or other white fish

1 tub (200g) cream cheese with chilli

Salt and pepper

Oven:

Simmering oven, 250F, 130C, Gas 1 and Roasting oven, 400F, 200C, Gas 6

Prepare in advance:

Keep in the fridge for up to 24 hours

Prepare ahead:

Keep warm in the simmering oven for an hour

Freeze:

Yes, defrost and reheat in roasting oven for half an hour

1   Set the milk for the topping in a jug on the back of the Aga to warm up. Set the tub of cream cheese onto the back of the Aga to warm up.

2   **For the topping:** Cut the potatoes and celeriac into even sized pieces and put into a pan. Cover with water and bring to the boil. Once they have boiled hard for a minute, drain, cover and put into the simmering oven for 30–40 minutes until soft.

3   Pour the warm milk onto the cooked potatoes and mash the potatoes with the butter, seasoning generously. Set aside to cool for a few minutes.

4   **For the base of the pie:** Cut the fish into 2"/5cm pieces and put into a wide ovenproof dish. Stir in the warm cream cheese.

5   Pile to potato onto the fish and make pretty patterns with a fork (or pipe it on if you are feeling really keen).

6   Set the grid shelf on the third set of runners and put the pie onto the shelf and cook for 25 – 40 minutes until golden brown and bubbling.

Aga tip: If there is any fish pie left over, mix together the remains and roll into balls to create fishcakes. Coat in seasoned flour then fry in a spoonful of rapeseed oil in a pan on the floor of the roasting oven

Aga tip: Warm milk makes much fluffier mashed potato, as long as you can remember to put it on the Aga when the potatoes go into the oven!

lemon chicken
with COUSCOUS

To feed more people: Cut the chicken breasts into small chunks to serve 5

Serves 4

4 boneless skinless chicken breasts

2 preserved lemons

1 tbsp rapeseed oil

1 clove garlic

½ tsp smoked paprika

8 oz (225g) wholemeal couscous

3 oz (85g) dried cranberries

½ pint (300ml) chicken stock

1 tin (400g) haricot beans

1 tbsp chopped parsley to finish

Oven:

Roasting oven, 200C, 400F, Gas 6

Prepare in advance:

Meat can sit in the marinade in the fridge for 24 hours

Prepare ahead:

Will keep warm in the simmering or warming oven for an hour or more

Freeze:

Yes, uncooked chicken in the marinade

1   Chop the preserved lemons and crush the garlic then mix these with the oil, garlic and paprika.

2   Smear this paste over the chicken breasts and leave to marinate for an hour or so if possible.

3   Line the shallow baking tray with Bake-O-Glide and lay the pieces of chicken into it. Hang the tin from the second runners in the roasting oven for about 20 minutes until the chicken breasts are cooked through.

4   While the chicken is in the oven, bring the stock to the boil and add the couscous, cranberries and beans. Cover and put into the simmering oven until the chicken is cooked.

5   Stir the couscous and serve the chicken on top of a pile of couscous, with a scattering of chopped parsley on top to show you have made an effort.

alsatian chicken

To feed more people: Two chickens and double the rest of the ingredients will feed 8 or 9, three chickens will feed up to 14

Serves 4

2 tbsp rapeseed oil

1 chicken, cut into 8 joints, or

8 joints of chicken

4 oz (110g) bacon

1 onion

1 clove garlic

1 tbsp fresh tarragon

1 tbsp plain flour

¼ pint (150ml) Alsace wine

¼ pint (150ml) chicken stock

Salt and pepper

3 tbsp crème fraîche

Oven:

Floor of roasting oven and

simmering oven, 130C, 250F,

Gas 1

Prepare in advance:

Cooked, cooled casserole will

keep in the fridge for up to

24 hours

Prepare ahead:

Will keep warm in the simmering

oven for an hour or so

Freeze:

Yes, defrost thoroughly and reheat in roasting oven

for half an hour

1   Peel and chop the onion, crush the garlic and snip the bacon into small pieces.

2   Heat the oil in the base of the rectangular roaster or 30cms buffet pan and add the chicken pieces, onion and bacon.

3   Set the pan onto the floor of the roasting oven to fry and brown for about 10 minutes, shaking the pan after 5 minutes.

4   Move the pan to the boiling plate, stir in the garlic, tarragon and flour, then add the wine and stock, stirring as it comes to the boil. Season, cover the pan with its lid and move to the simmering oven for about an hour.

5   When the meat is cooked, move the pan to the simmering plate, stir in the crème fraîche and bring to the boil.

6   If the sauce is a bit runny, put the pan back onto the floor of the roasting oven to boil and reduce.

7   Serve with new potatoes and a green vegetable.

john barleycorn chicken

To feed more people: Double the ingredients will feed 8 people, maybe 10 if served with mashed potatoes and a green vegetable

Serves 4

8 oz (half a pint in a measuring jug) (225g) pearl barley

1 medium onion

2 cloves garlic

½" (1cm) piece fresh ginger

1 red chilli

2 tbsp rapeseed oil

1 pint (550ml) chicken stock

1 lb (450g) chicken thigh meat

Salt and pepper

Parsley to garnish

Oven:

Aga simmering oven, 130C, 250F, Gas 1

Prepare in advance:

Cooked, cooled dish will keep in fridge for 24 hours

Prepare ahead:

Will keep warm for an hour in the simmering oven

Freeze:

Yes, defrost and reheat in roasting oven for half an hour

1   Peel and chop the onion and ginger, crush the garlic and chop the chilli. Cut the chicken into 2"/5cms chunks.

2   Heat the oil in a heavy pan on the simmering plate, and add the chicken, onion, ginger, chilli and garlic. When sizzling, transfer to the floor of the roasting oven for 10 minutes, shaking the pan occasionally to brown the meat evenly.

3   Transfer the pan to the simmering plate and stir in the pearl barley, seasoning and stock. Bring to the boil, then cover and put into the simmering oven for at least 20 minutes.

4   Serve with a scattering of chopped parsley

chicken veronique

To feed more people: Double the ingredients will feed 8 easily, if you cut up the meat it will feed 9 – 10. 12 sliced chicken breasts will feed up to 16

Serves 4

4 boneless, skinless chicken breasts

1 tbsp rapeseed oil

1 onion

1 clove garlic

6 oz (175g) green grapes

2 tbsp natural yogurt

2 tbsp dry white Vermouth or wine

Salt and pepper

Oven:

Roasting oven, 200C, 400F, Gas 6 and simmering oven 130C, 250F, Gas 1

Prepare in advance:

Prepared and cooked sauce will keep in the fridge for 24 hours

Prepare ahead:

Will keep warm in the simmering or warming oven for an hour

Freeze:

Not the grapes!

1 Peel and chop the onion and crush the garlic, halve the grapes (optional, but it looks as if you have made a bit of an effort!)

2 Line a shallow baking tray with Bake-O-Glide.

3 Heat the oil in a pan on the boiling plate and add the onions and garlic. Cover with a lid and when the lid is too hot to rest your hand on comfortably, transfer the pan to the simmering oven for about 15 minutes for the onions to soften.

4 Lay the chicken breasts onto the tray and hang it from the 2nd runners in the roasting oven for about 20 minutes until the meat is cooked.

5 When the meat is cooked, remove the tray from the oven and leave the meat to rest while you put together the sauce.

6 Take the pan of onions from the oven and put it onto the simmering plate. Stir in the grapes, wine and yogurt. Season well.

7 Serve the meat with the sauce poured over, accompanied by some rice or pasta.

chicken with lentils and mustard

To feed more people: Cut the meat into smaller pieces and add some extra lentils to feed one more, or double the ingredients to feed 9

Serves 4

1lb (450g) boneless, skinless chicken thighs

1 onion

1 clove garlic

1 tbsp rapeseed oil

8 oz (225g) green lentils (e.g. Puy)

1 pint (550ml) stock

4 tbsp white Vermouth

2 tbsp natural yogurt

1 tbsp French mustard

Oven:

Floor of roasting oven, simmering oven, 130C, 250F, Gas 1

Prepare in advance:

Cooked, cooled dish will keep in the fridge for 24 hours

Prepare ahead:

Will keep warm in the simmering or warming oven for an hour or so

Freeze:

Yes

1   Cut the chicken thighs into three pieces each. Peel and chop the onion, crush the garlic.

2   Heat the oil in a heavy pan and add the chicken, onion and garlic. Shake the pan over the boiling plate to warm it up, then transfer to the floor of the roasting oven for about 10 minutes for the meat to brown and the onions to soften.

3   Move the pan to the boiling plate and add the lentils, Vermouth and stock. Bring to the boil, then cover and move to the simmering oven for about 45 minutes until the lentils are soft.

4   Stir the yogurt and mustard into the lentil mixture and serve.

chicken and vegetable all in one bake

To feed more people: Double the ingredients will fill two roasting tins (do not cover in the oven and swap the tins over half way through cooking to make sure they both brown). This will feed up to 10.

Serves 4

1 chicken, about 1.5kg or 8 chicken pieces

4 medium potatoes

4 carrots

2 onions

2 cloves garlic

2 leeks

2 sticks celery

2 tbsp rapeseed oil

1 tbsp smoked paprika

1 tbsp garam masala

1 tsp celery salt

Oven:

Roasting oven, 200C, 400F, Gas 6

Prepare in advance:

Assemble the dish, cover and keep in the fridge for 24 hours before cooking - as long as the potatoes are coated in the oil they should not go brown

Prepare ahead:

Will keep warm in the simmering or warming oven for another hour

Freeze:

Don't see why not!

1 Joint the chicken into 8 pieces (or buy 8 pieces of chicken!)

2 Line the large roasting tin with Bake-O-Glide.

3 Peel and quarter the onions, crush the garlic, cut the carrots, leeks, celery and potatoes into even sized chunks, about 2″/5cm long and tip everything into the tin. Pour the oil over and shake to combine.

4 Lay the chicken pieces on top of the vegetables.

5 Mix together the spices and scatter over the chicken and vegetables.

6 Put a piece of Bake-O-Glide or foil over the top of the chicken.

7 Hang the tin from the 3rd runners in the roasting oven and bake for about half an hour.

8 Remove the Bake-O-Glide and shake the tin, then return it to the oven for another half hour until the vegetables are tender and the chicken pieces browned and cooked through.

9 Serve with a scattering of chopped parsley to show you have made an effort.

chicken noodle sauté

To feed more people: Double the ingredients will cook in the preserving pan and should serve up to 10, if on smallish plates

Serves 4

1lb (450g) chicken meat – thighs or breasts, cut into strips about 1˝/2½ cms wide

Marinade:

Salt and black pepper

2 cloves garlic

3 tbsp rapeseed oil

3 tbsp sweet chilli sauce

2 tbsp dark muscovado sugar

1 tbsp dark soy sauce

1 tbsp rice vinegar

Noodles:

3 heads pak choi

8 oz (225g) rice noodles

½ tin (200g) coconut milk

3 tbsp sweet chilli sauce

2 tbsp rice vinegar

2 tbsp dark muscovado sugar

3 cloves garlic

1 bunch spring onions

Bunch fresh coriander

3 tbsp peanuts, plus more for topping

2 tbsp Thai basil leaves

3 tbsp sesame oil

lime wedges for serving

Oven:

Floor of roasting oven, boiling plate

Prepare in advance:

Meat will sit in its marinade in the fridge overnight, prepare all other ingredients but cook and assemble at the last minute

Prepare ahead:

Not really, needs to be eaten as soon as it is ready

Freeze:

Not really, needs to be eaten as soon as it is ready

1   First make the marinade – mix everything together and pour over the chicken meat. Leave to stand for at least an hour, or put into the fridge overnight.

2   For the noodles, peel and crush the garlic, separate the pak choi leaves, trim and slice the spring onions and chop the peanuts and herbs. Boil the kettle.

3   Heat a sauté pan in the roasting oven then add the chicken and its marinade. Set the pan onto the floor of the roasting oven and leave to brown for about 5 minutes, then shake the meat in the pan and brown on the other side for a further 5 minutes – the marinade will caramelise and darken.

4   While the meat is in the oven, pour the boiling water over the noodles in a large pan and set onto the boiling plate and cook for as long as the pack instructs. Drain and leave in the pan to keep warm.

5   When the chicken meat is cooked, move the pan to the boiling plate and add the coconut milk, chilli sauce, rice vinegar, sugar, garlic and spring onions.

6   When this is boiling, stir in the cooked drained noodles, pak choi, herbs, sesame oil and peanuts. Stir to combine then serve.

chicken biryani

To feed more people: Double the ingredients will stretch around 10, or add double the rice and stock to feed a gang of hungry teenagers

Serves 4 – 5

1½ lb (650g) chicken breasts

3 onions

1" (2½ cms) piece fresh ginger

2 cloves garlic

2 tbsp rapeseed oil

8 oz (half a pint in a measuring jug) (225g) basmati rice

¾ pint (450ml) chicken stock

½ tsp ground cinnamon

1 tsp ground turmeric

5 cardamom pods

2 cloves

1 tsp ground cumin

Oven:

Floor of roasting oven and simmering oven, 130C, 250F, Gas 1

Prepare in advance:

Cooked, cooled biryani will keep in the fridge for 24 hours

Prepare ahead:

Will keep warm in the simmering or warming oven for an hour or so

Freeze:

Yes, defrost and reheat in the centre of the roasting oven for about 30 minutes

1   Cut the meat into even sized chunks.

2   Peel and slice the onions, peel and chop the ginger and chop the garlic.

3   Heat the oil in a heavy based pan and add the meat and vegetables. When the pan is sizzling, transfer it to the floor of the roasting oven for about 5 minutes until the meat has browned.

4   Put the spices into a mortar and bash with a pestle, then remove the cardamom husks.

5   Move the pan of meat to the boiling plate and stir in the spices. Add the rice and stock, then bring to the boil.

6   When the pan is boiling, cover with a lid and transfer to the simmering oven for 15 – 150 minutes.

7   Serve with a scattering of chopped coriander to show you have made an effort.

jambalaya

To feed more people: Double the ingredients will feed up to 9

Serves 4

2 tbsp rapeseed oil

12 oz (375g) chicken thighs

3 oz (85g) chorizo

2 sticks celery

1 onion

1 clove garlic

1 tbsp sun dried tomato purée

2 tsp Cajun spice mix

8 oz (225g) ½ pint in a measuring jug) long grain rice

¾ pint (450ml) chicken stock

Salt and pepper

3 tomatoes

6 oz (175g) raw prawns

Oven:

Simmering oven, 130C, 250F, Gas 1

Prepare in advance:

Cooked, cooled jambalaya will keep in the fridge for up to 24 hours

Prepare ahead:

Will keep warm in the simmering or warming oven for an hour or so

Freeze:

Yes

1 Cut the chicken thighs into 1"/2cm chunks, slice the chorizo. Peel and chop the onion and celery and crush the garlic.

2 Heat the oil in a heavy-based pan and add the meat and vegetables (not the tomatoes at this stage!) Move the pan to the floor of the roasting oven to fry and brown for about 10 minutes, shaking the pan after 5 minutes.

3 Move the pan to the boiling plate and stir in the spices and tomato purée. Add the rice and stock and bring to the boil. Cover and put into the simmering oven for about 20 minutes.

4 Chop the tomatoes and add them to the pan, with the prawns. Stir, re-cover and leave the pan to stand for 5 minutes – the heat of the rice will cook the prawns.

5 Serve.

sichuan gunpowder chicken

To feed more people: Double the ingredients will feed up to 9, triple the chicken and double the sauce will feed 14

Serves 4

8 boneless, skinless chicken thighs (about two packs), or a whole small chicken, jointed

2 tbsp soy sauce

2 tbsp vegetable oil

5 whole dried red chillies

2 tsp Sichuan peppercorns

10 spring onions

2 cloves garlic

2 oz (55g) roasted cashew nuts

Sauce:

5 tbsp soy sauce

2 tbsp rice wine

4 tbsp Chinese black vinegar

4 tbsp chicken stock

2 tsp soft brown sugar

1 tbsp cornflour

1 tbsp water

2 tbsp chopped fresh coriander

Oven:

Boiling plate

Prepare in advance:

Marinate the chicken overnight, prepare all the ingredients 24 hours in advance but stir fry at the last minute

Prepare ahead:

Will keep warm in the simmering or warming oven for half an hour

Freeze:

Don't see why not!

1　Cut the chicken pieces into 1"/2cm chunks and put into a non-metallic dish. Pour over the 2 tbsp soy sauce and allow to marinate for an hour or two. Wash and trim the spring onions, slice into ½"/1cm pieces. Crush the garlic.

2　Mix together the sauce ingredients and keep to one side.

3　Heat a heavy based sauté pan in the roasting oven for 5 minutes.

4　Transfer the pan to the boiling plate and add the vegetable oil. Tip the chicken meat into the pan and stir fry until the meat has changed colour and starts to caramelise around the edges – about 8 minutes.

5　Cut the tops off the chillies and tip out the seeds, which may be rather hot. Crush the Sichuan peppercorns with the garlic, and add this mixture, with the chillies, to the pan. Stir fry for a minute, then add the spring onions and nuts.

6　Tip the sauce mixture into the pan and stir fry until it has thickened. Serve at once, with a scattering of chopped coriander to show you have made an effort and some rice or noodles.

tarragon chicken salad

To feed more people: Two large chickens will feed up to 14, especially if part of a bigger salad buffet

Serves 5–6

3lb (1.5kg) chicken

3 tbsp fresh tarragon

4 spring onions

Bunch watercress

Dressing:

2 tbsp rapeseed oil

1 tbsp cider vinegar

¼ pint (150ml) natural yogurt

Salt and pepper

Oven:

Simmering oven, 130C, 250F,

Gas 1

Prepare ahead:

Cooked, cooled chicken will keep in the fridge for up to 24 hours

Finished salad will keep in the fridge for 4 hours

Freeze:

No

1 To cook the chicken – <u>either a</u>. Put it into a casserole with a tight fitting lid and maybe a chopped onion, cover and put into the simmering oven for 3–4 hours <u>or b</u>. Bring a large pan of water to the boil, put in the chicken, a chopped onion, some carrots and some parsley stalks, bring back to the boil then cover and put into the simmering oven for an hour. Take the chicken from the oven and allow to cool completely.

2 Remove the chicken from the bones and cut into ¾"/2cm pieces.

3 Trim and slice the spring onions.

4 Chop the tarragon finely, then mix with all the dressing ingredients.

5 Stir together the chicken, spring onions, and dressing.

6 Arrange the watercress on a plate, pile the chicken mixture onto it and serve, garnished with some more tarragon.

sticky chinese chicken

To feed more people: Double the ingredients will feed up to 9, especially if the thighs are halved. Triple the main ingredients and double the sauce will feed up to 14; bake in the large roasting tin

Serves 4

8 chicken thigh joints

8 oz (225g) carrots

3 cloves garlic

2 large onions

2 oz (55g) cashew nuts

1 tbsp chopped fresh coriander to serve

Sauce:

4 tbsp runny honey

4 tbsp bought chilli dipping sauce

1 lime

1 orange

1 tbsp rice vinegar

1 tbsp sundried tomato purée

1 lump stem ginger

Oven:

Roasting oven, 200C, 400F, Gas 6

Prepare in advance:

Cooked, cooled dish will keep in the fridge for 24 hours, reheat in the roasting oven for 20 minutes

Prepare ahead:

Will keep warm in the simmering or warming oven for up to an hour

Freeze:

Don't see why not!

1   Peel the onions and garlic. Cut the carrots and onions into chunks and halve the garlic cloves.

2   Mix together the chicken meat and vegetables with the oil. Tip into a shallow baking tray and hang from the 3rd runners in the roasting oven for about 20 minutes.

3   **For the sauce:** grate the rind from the fruit and squeeze the juice. Grate the ginger and mix all the ingredients.

4   Pour the sauce over the chicken and return to the oven for another 10–15 minutes, until it is sticky and browned.

5   Scatter the cashews and coriander over the cooked chicken and serve with Aga rice.

saffron chicken

To feed more people: Two chickens and double the rest of the ingredients will feed 8 or 9, three chickens will feed up to 14

Serves 4

2 tbsp rapeseed oil

1 chicken, cut into 8 joints, or 8 joints of chicken

2 onions

2 cloves garlic

Pinch fresh saffron

1 glass (125ml) dry sherry

1 tbsp plain flour

¼ pint (150ml) chicken stock

Salt and pepper

2 sprigs fresh thyme

2 oz (55g) raisins

2 tbsp pine nuts

Oven:

Floor of roasting oven and simmering oven, 130C, 250F, Gas 1

Prepare in advance:

Cooked, cooled casserole will keep in the fridge for up to 24 hours

Prepare ahead:

Will keep warm in the simmering oven for an hour or so

Freeze:

Yes, defrost thoroughly and reheat in roasting oven for half an hour

1   Put the stock into a pan and bring to the boil. Add the saffron threads and remove from the heat.

2   Peel and chop the onion, crush the garlic.

3   Heat the oil in a large pan and add the chicken pieces, onion and garlic.

4   Set the pan onto the floor of the roasting oven to fry and brown for about 10 minutes, shaking the pan after 5 minutes.

5   Move the pan to the boiling plate, stir in the raisins and flour, then add the sherry, thyme and stock, stirring as it comes to the boil. Season, cover and move to the simmering oven for about an hour.

6   When the meat is cooked, stir in the pine nuts.

7   If the sauce is a bit runny, put the pan back onto the floor of the roasting oven to boil and reduce.

8   Serve with rice and a green vegetable.

crimson chicken

To feed more people: Double the ingredients will feed up to 9

Serves 4

8 chicken thigh joints

1 red onion

½" (1cm) fresh ginger

1 clove garlic

2 large beetroot

2 tbsp rapeseed oil

1 tbsp plain flour

2 tbsp dry white Vermouth

½ pint (300ml) stock

Salt and pepper

Oven:

Floor of roasting oven and
simmering oven, 130C, 250F,
Gas 1

Prepare in advance:

Will keep in the fridge for up to
24 hours

Prepare ahead:

Will keep warm in the simmering
or warming oven for an extra hour
or two

Freeze:

Yes.

1   If using raw, fresh beetroot, put them, whole, into the
    roasting oven for half an hour. Remove from the oven,
    trim the leaves off and allow to cool.

2   Peel and chop the onion, crush the garlic and chop
    the ginger.

3   Heat the oil in a large casserole and add the onions,
    ginger and garlic. Add the chicken thigh joints.
    Transfer the pan to the floor of the roasting oven for
    10 minutes to brown the meat.

4   Grate the beetroot – use a processor or put rubber
    gloves on, or you will have purple hands for a week.

5   Move the pan to the simmering plate and add the
    flour, grated beetroot, Vermouth and stock. Stir until it
    comes to the to the boil and then cover the pan and
    put it into the simmering oven for about half an hour,
    or up to two hours.

6   Serve with Aga rice and a green vegetable.

Aga tip: The smaller the pieces of meat, the faster they will cook. If you are planning to
leave this in the oven all afternoon, keep the thighs whole, if you want it to be ready in half
an hour, cut the meat into small pieces

sticky chicken balls

To feed more people: Double the mixture will feed up to 9, three times the mixture with double the sauce will feed up to 14

Serves 4

1lb (450g) boneless, skinless chicken thighs

1 onion

1 carrot

1 lemon

Sauce:

3oz (100ml) mirin

3 tbsp soy sauce

3 tbsp caster sugar

Juice of the lemon

Oven:

Roasting oven, 200C, 400F, Gas 6

Prepare in advance:

Raw chicken balls will keep in the fridge for 24 hours, cooked, cooled balls will keep in the fridge for 24 hours

Prepare ahead:

Will keep warm in the simmering or warming oven for an hour

Freeze:

Raw chicken balls only

1 Peel and chop the onion, grate the zest from the lemon and squeeze the juice.

2 Put the onion, carrot, lemon zest and chicken into a processor and whizz to a paste. Season with salt and pepper.

3 Line the small shallow baking tray with Bake-O-Glide.

4 Roll spoonsful of the chicken mixture into balls and set onto the baking tray.

5 Hang the tin from the 3rd runners in the roasting oven and cook for about 10 minutes until browned.

6 Meanwhile, put the mirin, soy sauce, sugar and lemon juice into a pan and set on the simmering plate to come to the boil.

7 Serve the chicken balls with rice and a green vegetable, with the sauce poured over.

north african
sweet chicken

To feed more people: Double the ingredients will feed up to 10

Serves 4

1 lb (450g) boneless, skinless chicken thighs

1 tbsp rapeseed oil

2 red onions

2 cloves garlic

2 medium carrots

4 preserved lemons

1 tsp ground cinnamon

1 tsp ground cumin

2 oz (55g) chopped dates

4 oz (110g) couscous

½ pint (300ml) chicken stock

Fresh mint to garnish

Oven:

Floor of roasting oven, then simmering oven, 130C, 250F, Gas 1

Prepare in advance:

Cooked, cooled chicken will keep in the fridge for 24 hours

Prepare ahead:

Will keep warm in the warming or simmering oven for an hour

Freeze:

Yes

1 Peel and chop the onions, crush the garlic and slice the carrots and preserved lemons. Cut the chicken thighs into chunks.

2 Heat the oil in a heavy pan on the boiling plate, and add the chicken meat, onions and garlic. Stir, then move the pan to the floor of the roasting oven for 10 minutes to brown the meat and soften the vegetables.

3 Move the pan to the boiling plate and add the remaining ingredients, then bring to the boil.

4 Cover the pan and put it into the simmering oven for about 20 minutes until the meat is tender and all the liquid has been absorbed.

5 Serve with a scattering of chopped mint.

marinated chicken thighs

To feed more people: Double the ingredients will feed up to 9, triple will feed 15

Serves 4

6 boneless, skinless chicken thighs

1 tbsp rapeseed oil

1 tsp ground fennel seeds

1 tsp ground cumin

1 tsp smoked paprika

1 clove garlic

1 tbsp red wine vinegar

Oven:

Roasting oven, 200C, 400F, Gas 1

Prepare in advance:

Marinate the chicken thighs for 24 hours before cooking

Prepare ahead:

Will keep warm in the simmering or warming oven for an hour

Freeze:

Yes, cooked or in the marinade

1 Cut the chicken thighs into 3 pieces each.

2 Mix together the rest of the ingredients in a non-metallic bowl and stir in the meat.

3 Leave to marinate for an hour, or overnight in the fridge or for a month in the freezer.

4 Tip the pieces of marinated chicken onto a shallow baking tray, lined with Bake-O-Glide.

5 Hang the tin from the second runners in the roasting oven and cook for about 20 minutes.

6 Serve with rice and salad, and a blob of garlic mayonnaise.

pineapple and pork rice

Serves 4

8 oz (1/2 pint in a measuring jug)
long grain rice

¾ pint water or stock

2 tbsp groundnut oil

8oz (225g) minced pork

2 tbsp light soy sauce

salt and pepper

2" / 4cms piece fresh ginger

6 tbsp spring onions

2 cloves garlic

1 tbsp sesame oil

1 small pineapple

(approximately 8oz/225g), peeled,

cored and chopped into 1cm/½in

pieces

Oven:

Simmering oven, 130C, 250F,
Gas 1 and boiling plate

Prepare ahead:

Will keep warm in simmering or warming oven for
half an hour

Freeze:

No

1   First, cook the rice – put the rice and water into a pan
and bring to the boil. Cover and transfer to the
simmering oven for at least 15 minutes.

2   Trim and chop the ginger, garlic and spring onions.

3   Heat a heavy sauté pan or casserole on the boiling
plate. Add the pork and transfer to the floor of the
roasting oven to fry for 10 minutes. Move the pan
back to the boiling plate and add the soy sauce, salt,
pepper, ginger, garlic and spring onions and stir-fry
for two minutes.

4   Add the cooked rice, mix well and return to the floor
of the roasting oven for another five minutes until the
rice is heated through and well mixed.

5   Stir in the sesame oil, add the pineapple pieces and
stir fry until the pineapple is heated through, but not
cooked. Serve at once.

goan pork and
potato curry

To feed more people: Double the ingredients will feed up to 9, or more if you add extra potatoes!

Serves 4

1½ lb (650g) pork shoulder

2 tbsp rapeseed oil

1 lb waxy potatoes (eg Charlotte)

1 pint (550ml) stock

Marinade:

1 tsp mustard seeds

1 tsp cumin seeds

1 tsp coriander seeds

2 cloves

1 large onion

2 cloves garlic

1" (2.5cms) piece ginger

1 tsp smoked paprika

½ tsp turmeric

½ tsp salt

Oven:

Floor of roasting oven then

simmering oven, 130C, 250F,

Gas 1

Prepare in advance:

Cooked, cooled curry will keep in

the fridge for 24 hours

Prepare ahead:

Will keep warm in the simmering or warming oven for an hour or so

Freeze:

Yes

1   First, make the marinade. Crush the seeds together, then tip into a processor with the peeled garlic, ginger and onion and the other spices and blend to a paste with a spoonful of water.

2   Cut the meat into 1" (2.5cms) chunks and put into a plastic bag with the marinade. Seal and leave to soak up the flavour for an hour, or overnight in the fridge.

3   Heat the oil in a heavy pan on the boiling plate and tip in the meat and its marinade. Stir, then transfer the pan to the floor of the roasting oven for about 15 minutes for the meat to brown.

4   Cut the potatoes into quarters.

5   Move the pan to the boiling plate, add the potatoes and stock and bring to the boil. Cover and transfer to the simmering oven for about 30 minutes until the potatoes are tender.

red braised
chinese pork belly

To feed more people: Double the ingredients will feed up to 9, triple will stretch around 14 as part of a Chinese buffet with lots of rice or noodles

Serves 4–6

2 lb (900g) pork belly strips

1 tbsp soy sauce

7 oz (200ml) rice wine

3½ oz (100ml) Chinese black vinegar

2 tbsp vegetable oil

1 medium onion

2 cloves garlic

1˝/2cm piece ginger

Pinch chilli flakes

5 oz (150g) light muscovado sugar

1 pint stock

To serve:

Sesame seeds

Bunch spring onions

Oven:

Floor of roasting oven, simmering oven, 130C, 250F, Gas 1

Prepare in advance:

Will keep in the fridge for up to 24 hours

Prepare ahead:

Keep warm in the simmering or warming oven for an hour or so

Freeze:

Yes

1   Cut the pork into 2"/5cm pieces. Add the soy sauce and rice wine and stir together. Leave to marinate for an hour or overnight.

2   Peel and finely chop the onion, garlic and ginger.

3   Heat the oil in a large heavy casserole on the boiling plate, then add the meat, onion, ginger and garlic. Transfer the pan to the floor of the roasting oven for 10 minutes to brown, shaking the pan after 5 minutes to turn the meat.

4   Once the meat has browned, put the pan onto the boiling plate and add the rice wine, black vinegar, sugar, stock and chilli flakes. Stir until boiling, then cover and move the pan to the simmering oven for at least 2 hours.

5   Take the pan from the simmering oven, remove the lid and put the pan onto the floor of the roasting oven for about 15 minutes, to reduce and thicken the sauce.

6   Serve on noodles or rice, with sesame seeds and finely chopped spring onions scattered over the top of the pork.

pulled pork

Serves 6–8

3–4 lb (1.6kg) shoulder of pork

2 tbsp salt

2 tbsp dark muscovado sugar

1 tbsp smoked paprika

Oven:

Simmering oven, 130C, 250F,

Gas 1

Prepare in advance:

The cooked, cooled meat actually

improves in the fridge overnight

Prepare ahead:

It's already been in the oven for 6

hours, why would you need to

keep it warm for any longer?

Freeze:

Yes

1 Pat the meat dry with a paper towel.

2 Mix together the salt, sugar and paprika and rub into the meat. Put the coated meat into the lid of an Aga buffet pan, or a roasting tin lined with enough foil to fold over the joint and completely seal it.

3 Put the pork into the simmering oven and cook for about 6 hours, until it's really soft. Pour off the juices and reserve.

4 Remove the lid from the pan and transfer the meat to the Roasting oven and cook the pork, uncovered, for 10–15 minutes to crisp up the crackling. Take out and leave to rest.

5 Remove the skin from the joint and set it onto the grill rack in the roasting tin. Hang the tin from the first runners in the roasting oven to brown and crackle, while you serve the meat.

6 Use two forks to pull the meat into shreds, and then add the rest of the seasoning with the juice from the pan or tin, and stir together.

spiced pork

To feed more people: Double the ingredients will feed 8 or 9

Serves 4

2 tbsp rapeseed oil

1½ lb (600g) pork shoulder

4 oz (110g) piece chorizo

1 onion

2 cloves garlic

1 tbsp plain flour

1 tin (400g) tomatoes

2 oz (55g) black olives

¼ pint (150ml) red wine

¼ pint (150ml) chicken stock

Salt and pepper

Oven:

Floor of roasting oven and simmering oven, 130C, 250F, Gas 1

Prepare in advance:

Cooked, cooled casserole will keep in the fridge for up to 24 hours

Prepare ahead:

Will keep warm in the simmering oven for an hour or so

Freeze:

Yes, defrost thoroughly and reheat in roasting oven for half an hour

1   Cut the pork into 1" (2½ cms) chunks. Peel and chop the onion, crush the garlic and cut the chorizo into small pieces.

2   Heat the oil in the base of the rectangular roaster or 30cms buffet pan and add the pork pieces, onion and chorizo.

3   Set the pan onto the floor of the roasting oven to fry and brown for about 10 minutes, shaking the pan after 5 minutes.

4   Move the pan to the boiling plate, stir in the garlic, tomatoes, olives and flour, then add the wine and stock, stirring as it comes to the boil. Season, cover the pan with its lid and move to the simmering oven for about an hour until the meat is tender.

5   If the sauce is a bit runny, put the pan back onto the floor of the roasting oven to boil and reduce.

6   Serve with new potatoes and a green vegetable.

bacon, pea and mushroom pudding

Serves 6

1½ lb (750g) piece smoked bacon
or gammon

1 tin (400g) black eyed peas

8 oz (225g) button mushrooms

1 onion

½ pt (275ml) white wine

1 tbsp vegetable stock powder

1 tbsp plain flour

Black pepper

Pastry:

4 oz (110g) suet

8 oz (230g) self raising flour

About ¼ pint (150ml) cold water

2 tbsp plain flour for rolling

Oven:

Simmering oven, 130C, 250F,
Gas 1

Prepare ahead:

Can sit for 12 hours in the
simmering oven!

Freeze:

No

1 First make the pastry: sift the self raising flour into a bowl and stir in the suet. Add cold water one tablespoon at a time, until you have a dough. Knead for 2 minutes until pliable, then roll out (in the plain flour) to approx 14" (35cm) round. Cut out a quarter-sized slice and line a 2pt (1 litre) pudding basin with the large section. Re-roll the remaining quarter into an 8" (20cm) round to make a lid for the pudding.

2 For the filling: Cut the bacon into 1"/2½cm cubes. Chop the onion. Halve the mushrooms. Drain the tin of peas. Put the plain flour and stock powder into a plastic bag with plenty of pepper (no need for salt as the bacon is salty enough). Toss the meat, mushrooms, peas and onion in the bag, then tip into the lined pudding basin. Pour the wine over the meat.

3 Moisten the rim of the pastry lining the bowl and lay on the pastry lid, pinching together the edges. Cover with cling film (or clip the lid onto the plastic bowl!).

4 Take a long piece of foil or cling film and fold lengthways into a long strip, which goes under the basin, to act as a handle. Fill a large saucepan with enough water to come about a third of the way up the sides of the bowl, and lower in the basin. Set the pan onto the boiling plate and bring to the boil. Cover with a lid and transfer to the simmering oven for at least 4 hours – or up to 6 hours.

5 To serve, lift out the pudding and wrap the bowl in a white linen napkin before bringing to the table.

cuban pork

To feed more people: Double the ingredients will feed up to 9, more if served with a lot of rice or mashed potatoes!

Serves 4

1 lb (450g) pork belly rashers, as lean as you can find

1 tbsp rapeseed oil

1 medium onion

2 cloves garlic

1 tsp cumin seeds

2 oranges

2 limes

Oven:

Floor of roasting oven, simmering oven, 130C, 250F, Gas 1

Prepare in advance:

Cooked, cooled stew will keep in the fridge for 24 hours

Prepare ahead:

Will keep warm in the simmering or warming oven for an hour or so

Freeze:

Yes

1   Peel and chop the onion, crush the garlic. Cut the pork rashers into 1" chunks.

2   Heat a heavy based sauté pan on the boiling plate and add the oil. Add the pork, onions, garlic and cumin and stir over the heat, then transfer the pan, uncovered, to the floor of the roasting oven to brown the meat for ten minutes, shaking the pan once or twice.

3   Grate the rind from the oranges and limes and squeeze the juice.

4   Move the pan of browned meat to the boiling plate, stir in the fruit zest and juice and stir until boiling. Cover the pan and move it to the simmering oven for at least half an hour, or up to two hours.

5   Serve with rice or mashed potatoes, and a scattering of chopped parsley to show you have made an effort.

pork and <u>ginger stir fry</u>

To feed more people: Double the ingredients should stretch around 9 people

Serves 4

4 nests medium egg noodles

2 tsp cornflour

2 tbsp light soy sauce

1 tbsp runny honey

1 tbsp rapeseed oil

1lb (450g) pork fillet

1" (2.5cms) piece fresh ginger

1 clove garlic

6 spring onions

1 red pepper

4 oz (110g) mangetout peas

1 tsp sesame seeds

1 tsp sesame oil

Oven:

Simmering oven, 130C, 250F, Gas 1 and boiling plate

Prepare in advance:

Chop all the ingredients and keep in the fridge, but do not cook until ready to eat.

Prepare ahead:

If this sits in the simmering or warming oven for long, the vegetables will lose their crunch.

Freeze:

No, this is a cook and eat straight away dish!

1 Trim and slice the spring onions, grate the ginger and garlic, chop the red pepper and halve the mangetout.

2 Mix together the cornflour, soy sauce and honey.

3 Put a sauté pan into the roasting oven to heat up.

4 Cut the pork into thin slices.

5 Bring a pan of water to the boil and add the noodles, stir, cover and put the pan into the simmering oven for 5 minutes.

6 Move the hot sauté pan to the boiling plate and heat the oil in it. Add the pork and stir fry for a couple of minutes, then tip in the prepared vegetables. Stir fry for another minute or two, then pour in the cornflour mixture, the sesame seeds and sesame oil. Stir until bubbling.

7 Drain the noodles and serve with the pork.

canton stir-fried pepper beef with mangetout

Serves 4

1lb (450g) lean beef steak

2 tsp light soy sauce

2 tsp Shaoxing rice wine or dry sherry

2 tsp sesame oil

Salt and pepper

2 tsp cornflour

1 red pepper

1 red onion

3 tbsp rapeseed oil

8oz (225g) mangetout

5 tbsp chicken stock

2 tbsp oyster sauce

Oven:

Boiling plate

Prepare ahead:

Cut up all the ingredients and marinade the beef, but do not stir fry until just before serving

Freeze:

No

1 Put a heavy sauté pan or casserole into the roasting oven to get very hot.

2 Cut the beef into thin slices 2"/ 5cms long then put in a bowl with the light soy sauce, rice wine, sesame oil, salt, pepper and cornflour. Mix well and then leave the beef to marinate for 20 minutes.

3 Cut the red pepper into 2"/ 5cm strips and peel and slice the onion.

4 Add the rapeseed oil and add the beef to the pan and stir-fry for three minutes.

5 Add the vegetables and stir-fry for two minutes, then add the stock and oyster sauce. Bring the mixture to the boil.

6 Turn on to a warm serving plate and serve at once.

beef with pistachios

To feed more people: Double the ingredients will feed up to 9, three times will spread round 14, more if you add a couple of extra handfuls of lentils at the same time as the beer etc.

Serves 4

1½ lb (700g) stewing steak

1 large onion

1 clove garlic

1 pint (550ml) best bitter

2 tbsp redcurrant or quince jelly

2 tbsp yellow split peas

4 oz (110g) shelled pistachio nuts

Ground black pepper

2 tbsp oil for frying

2 tbsp plain flour

1 tbsp chopped parsley

Oven:

Floor of roasting oven, simmering oven, 130C, 250F, Gas 1

Prepare in advance:

Cooked, cooled stew will keep in the fridge for up to 48 hours

Prepare ahead:

Stew will keep warm in the simmering or warming oven for an additional hour or two

Freeze:

Yes

1 Cut the meat into 1"/2½cm cubes. Chop the onion. Peel and crush the garlic.

2 Put the flour, salt and pepper into a plastic bag and add the meat. Toss to coat evenly.

3 Heat the oil in a casserole pan and add the meat, onion and garlic. Transfer the pan to the floor of the roasting oven for 5 minute to brown. Shake the pan and return it to the floor of the oven for a further 5 minutes.

4 Transfer the pan to the boiling plate and add the split peas, beer and jelly and bring to the boil, stirring. Season and cover, then move to the simmering oven for about 2 hours.

5 Just before serving, stir in the nuts and serve sprinkled with parsley, with mashed potatoes and a green vegetable.

mince and tomato pie
with quinoa

To feed more people: Double the quantity will feed 8 easily, 9 if you serve it onto small plates! Three times the quantity will make a big pie for 12–14 in the large roasting tin

Serves 4

1lb (450g) beef mince

1 onion

1 clove garlic

3 carrots

1lb (450g) tomatoes

1 tsp smoked paprika

Salt and pepper

Topping:

½ pint in a mug (300ml) quinoa

1 pint stock

3 oz Cheddar cheese

Oven:

Simmering oven, 130C, 250F, Gas 1 and roasting oven, 200C, 400F, Gas 6 or a grill

Prepare in advance:

Assembled, cooled pie will keep in the fridge for 24 hours before cooking at the top of the roasting oven for 25 minutes to reheat and brown

Prepare ahead:

Will keep warm in the simmering or warming oven for an hour or two

Freeze:

Yes, assembled and before final browning

1   Peel and chop the onion, crush the garlic and chop the carrots into chunks. Chop the tomatoes into chunks.

2   Heat a sauté pan on the boiling plate and add the onion, garlic, carrots and mince. Stir over the heat for a minute, then transfer to the floor of the roasting oven for 5 – 8, minutes to brown.

3   Move the pan of browned mince to the boiling plate and stir in the tomatoes and paprika. Season well. When the contents of the pan are boiling, cover and transfer to the simmering oven for about 20 minutes or up to an hour or two.

4   Meanwhile, measure the quinoa and stock into a pan, bring to the boil cover and move to the simmering oven for about half an hour.

5   When the mince has cooked, take the pan from the oven and remove the lid.

6   Grate the cheese into the pan of quinoa and stir well. Spread the quinoa and cheese mixture over the top of the mince.

7   Slide the grid shelf onto the 2nd runners in the roasting oven and put the sauté pan onto it and bake for about 15 minutes until browned and crisp on top.

8   Serve with a green vegetable.

celebration fillet
of beef

Serves 6–8 – this is such a treat it needs to be served in generous portions

To feed more people: Cook two fillets to feed up to 18, or 20 if sliced thinly but what is the point of thinly sliced beef fillet?

1 whole fillet of beef, approx. 3lb (1.5kg)

1 tbsp rapeseed oil

2 cloves garlic

Salt and pepper

Oven:

Roasting oven, 220C, 450F, Gas 7

Prepare in advance:

Cook the joint in the morning and leave the meat to cool down but do not refrigerate and serve that evening. If serving cold with salad, allow plenty of time for the meat to come to room temperature before eating

Prepare ahead:

Will keep warm on the back of the Aga as it cools from roasting hot to tepid

Freeze:

No, roast fillet is far too nice to eat from the freezer!

1 Take the beef from the fridge at least an hour before you want to cook it, so that it is at room temperature.

2 Peel and crush the garlic.

3 Smear the meat with the oil, then rub it with the salt, pepper and garlic.

4 Slide the plain shelf into the roasting oven on the 4th runners, to trap the heat at the top of the oven and raise the temperature as much as possible. Wait 10 minutes for the heat at the top of the oven to build up.

5 Lay the meat onto the grill rack, on its high setting, and set the rack into a shallow baking tray (lined with Bake-O-Glide, of course). *This allows the heat to circulate all around the meat, like spit roasting without any movement.*

6 Hang the tin from the second runners in the roasting oven, so that it is as high as it can go in the oven.

7 Roast for about 40 minutes for rare, 50 minutes for medium rare.

8 Take the meat from the oven and leave to rest for at least 15 minutes before carving.

I like this served slightly warmer than tepid, with hollandaise (see p. 176) or heart attack sauce (see p. 178) with roast potatoes, and all the trimmings of course, or cold (but not refrigerated) with hot new potatoes and salad and a horseradish mayonnaise.

chilli con carne

To feed more people: Double the ingredients will feed up to 9, three times will spread round 14, or more if you add an extra can of beans or two

Serves 4

1½ lb (700g) stewing steak

2 tbsp plain flour

2 large onions

1 clove garlic

1 red chilli

2 dried smoked red chillies

½ pint (300ml) best bitter

1 tin (400g) chopped tomatoes

1 tin (400g) black eyed peas

2 squares plain chocolate

1 tsp smoked paprika (or more if you prefer)

Salt and pepper

2 tbsp rapeseed oil for frying

1 tbsp chopped parsley

Oven:

Floor of roasting oven, simmering oven, 130C, 250F, Gas 1

Prepare in advance:

Cooked, cooled stew will keep in the fridge for up to 48 hours

Prepare ahead:

Stew will keep warm in the simmering or warming oven for an additional hour or two

Freeze:

Yes

1 Cut the meat into 1"/2½cm cubes. Chop the onion and red chilli. Peel and crush the garlic. Open the tin of beans and drain it.

2 Fill the kettle with fresh water and set it onto the boiling plate to come to the boil.

3 Crumble the dried chillies into a jug and pour over quarter of a pint (150ml) of boiling water.

4 Put the flour, salt and pepper into a plastic bag and add the meat. Toss to coat evenly.

5 Heat the oil in a casserole pan and add the meat, onion, chilli and garlic. Transfer the pan to the floor of the roasting oven for 5 minutes to brown. Shake the pan and return it to the floor of the oven for a further 5 minutes.

6 Transfer the pan to the boiling plate and stir in the smoked paprika, then add the dried chillies and their soaking water, beer, drained beans and chocolate and bring to the boil, stirring occasionally. Cover and move to the simmering oven for about 2 hours.

7 Serve sprinkled with parsley, with Aga rice and a bowl of soured cream with chives chopped into it and a green vegetable or some salad.

cheat's meatloaf

To feed more people: Double the mixture will fill a 2lb /1kg loaf tin or a shallow loaf in the small roasting tin and will feed up to 10 with lots of mashed potato and tomato sauce

Serves 4

1 x packet (130g) dried stuffing mix – *I use supermarket posh range smoked sage and red onion*

1 lb (450g) lean pork mince

½ pint (300ml) stock

Oven:

Roasting oven, 200C, 400F, Gas 6

Prepare in advance:

Prepared, uncooked loaf will keep in the fridge for 24 hours

Prepare ahead:

Will keep warm in the simmering or warming oven for an hour

Freeze:

Yes

1 Bring the stock to the boil, then add the stuffing and mix well.

2 Leave to stand for 5 minutes for the dried ingredients to reconstitute.

3 Stir the mince into the stuffing.

4 Line a 1 lb / 500g loaf tin with Bake-O-Glide and press the mixture into it.

5 Set the loaf tin into the small roasting tin and hang from the 3rd runners in the roasting oven.

6 Bake for about 25 minutes until browned on top.

7 Serve with a tomato sauce.

duck with orange and cranberries

To feed more people: Slice the duck breasts before putting them onto 5 or even 6 plates if they are really big. 8 duck breasts should stretch around 12 people, but will need cooking in batches unless you have a really massive griddle pan

Serves 4

  4 duck breasts

  4 tbsp Marsala or Madeira

  ¼ pint (150ml) stock

  1 orange

  3 oz (75g) cranberries

  2 tbsp orange marmalade

  Salt and pepper

Oven:

  Floor of roasting oven

Prepare in advance:

  Make the sauce in advance, but the meat is nicest eaten on the day it is cooked

Prepare ahead:

  Will keep warm in the simmering or warming oven for an hour, but the meat will no longer be as pink

Freeze:

  No, the meat toughens as it is reheated

1 Put a heavy griddle pan into the roasting oven to heat up for 5 minutes.

2 Remove the skin from the duck breasts if you are feeling slim (or not too slim!)

3 Put the meat into the pan, skin side down (if you have left the skin on) and return it to the floor of the roasting oven for 5–10 minutes to brown and cook.

4 When the meat is browned, move the pan to the simmering plate and turn the pieces of meat over. Grate the orange zest on top, then squeeze the juice over. Add the Marsala and stock, cranberries and marmalade. Season and stir.

5 Put the pan back onto the floor of the oven for a further 5 minutes for the meat to continue cooking and for the sauce to bubble and reduce.

6 Serve the duck in slices, with the sauce poured over and some potatoes and a green vegetable.

Aga tip: Griddling the duck breasts on the floor of the oven means that any fat spitting from the pan will disappear up the flue, so there will be no mess on the top of the cooker

bambi goes east

To feed more people: Double the ingredients will feed 8 or 9, three times the meat and double the sauce will feed up to 12

Serves 4

1½ lb (650g) stewing venison

1 medium onion

2 cloves garlic

1" (2.5 cms) piece ginger

1 stalk lemongrass

1 green chilli

1 tsp sugar

½ tsp salt

1 tbsp rapeseed oil

1 tbsp plain flour

1 tbsp soy sauce

½ pint (300ml) stock

Oven:

Simmering oven, 130C, 250F, Gas 1

Prepare in advance:

Cooked, cooled casserole will keep in the fridge for 24 hours

Prepare ahead:

Will keep warm in the simmering or warming oven for an hour or two

Freeze:

Yes

1 Peel the onion, garlic and ginger.

2 Put the onion, garlic, ginger, lemongrass, chilli, sugar, and salt into a processor and whizz to a paste.

3 Heat the oil in a heavy pan on the simmering plate and add the paste. Stir over the heat until it sizzles, then stir in the flour, soy sauce and stock.

4 Add the meat to the sauce and bring to the boil. Cover and transfer the pan to the simmering oven for at least two hours.

5 Serve with rice and a green vegetable.

sausage and
chestnut casserole

To feed more people: Double the ingredients will feed 8 or 9, three times the meat and double the sauce will feed up to 12

Serves 4 – 5

2 lb (2 x 450g pack) sausages

1 onion

1 clove garlic

1 tbsp oil

4 oz (110g) bacon pieces

1 pack (200g) prepared chestnuts

1 tbsp Dijon mustard

½ oz (10g) plain flour

½ pint (300ml) stock

Salt and pepper

Oven:

Roasting oven, simmering oven, 130C, 250F, Gas 1

Prepare in advance:

Cooked cooled casserole will keep in the fridge for 24 hours

Prepare ahead:

Will keep warm in the warming or simmering oven for an extra hour or two

Freeze:

Yes

1   Peel and chop the onion and crush the garlic. Separate the sausages – you could cut them into halves or thirds to make them look more on the plate.

2   Heat a large casserole on the boiling plate and add the oil, sausages, onion, garlic and bacon pieces.

3   When the contents of the pan are sizzling, transfer it to the floor of the roasting oven, uncovered, to brown the meat for 10 minutes, shaking the pan once or twice.

4   Take the pan of browned sausages from the oven and set it onto the boiling plate. Stir in the flour and mustard, then add the stock and stir well. Tip in the prepared chestnuts and once it is boiling, cover the pan and move it to the simmering oven for at least half an hour, up to 3 hours.

5   Serve with mashed potatoes and a green vegetable.

sausage and
pepper casserole

To feed more people: Double the ingredients will feed up to 12

Serves 6 – 8

2lb (900g) nice sausages

1 tbsp rapeseed oil

2 onions

2 cloves garlic

1 tin (400g) butter beans

1 tin (400g) haricot beans

2 tins (400g each) chopped

tomatoes

10 peppadew peppers

½ pint (300ml) red wine

2 tbsp grated Parmesan cheese

Oven:

Floor of roasting oven, simmering
oven, 130C, 250F, Gas 1

Prepare in advance:

Cooked, cooled casserole will
keep in the fridge for 24 hours

Prepare ahead:

Will keep warm in the simmering
or warming oven for an hour or
two

Freeze:

Yes

1   Cut the sausages into ½"/1cm slices. Put the
    sausages into a frying pan and put it onto the floor of
    the roasting oven for about 15 minutes.

2   Peel and chop the onions, crush the garlic and chop
    the peppers. Open the tins, draining the beans.

3   Heat the oil in a heavy based casserole and add the
    onions, garlic and peppers. Put the lid on and, when
    sizzling, transfer to the simmering oven for about 15
    minutes to soften.

4   Move the casserole of softened onions to the boiling
    plate, then tip in the tins of beans and tomatoes,
    together with the wine. Season well and bring to the
    boil.

5   Take the pan of browned sausages from the roasting
    oven and, using a slotted spoon, lift the sausages
    from their fat. Put the meat into the casserole and stir.
    Cover and put into the simmering oven for half an
    hour, or an hour, or two hours.

6   Just before eating, stir in the Parmesan.

7   Serve with baked potatoes or crusty bread and a
    green vegetable.

lentejas — spanish lentil stew

This looks like a vast list of ingredients, but as you just put it all into a pan and bung it in the oven, it is not the hard work the list implies

Serves 4

9 oz (250 g) green lentils

1 chorizo sausage in a piece (200g)

3½ oz (100g) serrano ham

1 large onion

1 small glass of red wine

2 cloves

1 red pepper

5 tbsp rapeseed oil

1 bayleaf

2 large carrots

3 small potatoes

2 cloves garlic

1 pinch of saffron

Fresh parsley

Salt and pepper

Oven:

Aga simmering oven, 130C, 250F, Gas 1, then floor of roasting oven

Prepare in advance:

Cooked cooled stew will keep in the fridge for 24 hours

Prepare ahead:

Will keep warm in simmering or warming oven for up to an hour

Freeze:

Yes.

1   Cut the ham and chorizo into dice-shaped pieces. Slice the carrots and cut the potatoes into 1" /2cm chunks. Wash and slice the red pepper. Peel and chop the onion and crush the garlic.

2   Slice the onion and garlic and tip into a sauté pan with the oil and set onto the boiling plate. After a minute or so, add the sliced red pepper. When soft, add the other ingredients to the saucepan. Put the pan onto the simmering plate and cover. When the lid is too hot to leave your hand on, move the pan to the simmering oven.

3   Let the lentil stew cook for at least 40 minutes. If there is too much liquid in the pan at the end of the cooking, remove the lid and transfer the pan to the floor of the roasting oven for 5 minutes to boil it off.

herb roasted lamb

Serves 4 – 6

3-4 lb (1.5-2kg) leg of lamb

2 tbsp natural yogurt

2 tbsp mixed fresh herbs –
parsley, tarragon, basil, thyme

1 clove garlic, crushed

Glass of red wine

1 tbsp plain flour

1 tbsp redcurrant jelly

½ pint (300ml) good stock

Salt and pepper

Oven:

Roasting oven, 200C, 400F, Gas 6

Prepare ahead:

Lamb joint will keep warm in
simmering oven for an extra hour
or so, but it will continue to cook a
little. Keep the gravy warm in a jug
on the back of the Aga

Freeze:

No

1 Line the small roasting tin with Bake-O-Glide.

2 Cut slashes into the lamb skin with a sharp knife so
that the coating flavours the meat as well as the skin.

3 Mix the chopped herbs and the garlic into the yogurt
and smear this all over the lamb and put it into the tin.
If time allows, leave this to marinate for an hour, or
cover and keep in the fridge overnight.

4 Hang the tin from the 3rd runners in the roasting oven
and roast for an hour, then move it to the simmering
oven and continue to cook for a further half an hour,
or two hours if you like . . .

5 When the lamb is cooked, remove it from the tin and
put onto a plate and leave to rest in the simmering or
warming oven while you make the sauce.

6 Tip away any excess fat in the tin, leaving about 2
tbsp, plus any crunchy bits from the lamb.

7 Add the flour and stir well, then tip in the wine,
redcurrant jelly and stock to the tin, season and mix
well.

8 Set the tin onto the floor of the roasting oven for 5
minutes until boiling and thickened.

9 Serve the lamb carved in slices, with a little gravy
poured over. Not forgetting the roast potatoes of
course!

lamb steaks with
mango sauce

Serves 4

4 lamb leg steaks

¼ pint red wine

2 tbsp mango chutney

2 cloves garlic

Salt and pepper

Oven:

Roasting oven, 400F, 200C, Gas 6

Prepare ahead:

Will keep warm in the simmering
or warming oven for 30 minutes

Freeze:

*Yes, but the meat will not be pink
when reheated*

1 Heat a large sauté pan in the roasting oven for 5
minutes. Transfer the pan to the boiling plate.

2 Lay the steaks into the pan, then move it onto the
floor of the roasting oven for 3 – 5 minutes
(depending whether you like the meat rare or
medium), then take out and turn the steaks over.
Return to the oven for a further 3 – 5 minutes.
Remove the steaks from the pan and leave to rest on
a plate in the simmering oven.

3 Crush the garlic and add to the meat juices in the
pan, together with the wine and mango chutney. Bring
to the boil on the simmering plate, then return it to the
floor of the roasting oven for 5 minutes, to boil and
reduce. Serve the sauce poured over the steaks.

Alternatives:

• Use venison steaks, with cranberry sauce instead of the mango chutney

• Use beef sirloin steaks and horseradish instead of the chutney

lamb and bacon stew

To feed more people: Double the quantity will feed up to 9, or 10 with a lot of rice and vegetables

Serves 4

3 bacon rashers

1 large onion

3 cloves garlic

1lb 4oz (500g) lamb neck fillet

1 tbsp rapeseed oil

3 tbsp white Vermouth

4 oz (110g) mushrooms

Salt and pepper

1 tbsp plain flour

Oven:

Simmering oven, 130C, 250F, Gas 1

Prepare in advance:

Cooked, cooled stew will keep in the fridge for 24 hours

Prepare ahead:

Will keep warm in the simmering or warming oven for a few hours

Freeze:

Yes

1 Slice the bacon and put in a large sauté pan.

2 Chop the onion and crush the garlic. Add to the pan with the oil.

3 Cut the lamb into cubes and add to the pan with the seasoning. Transfer the pan to the floor of the roasting oven for about 10 minutes to brown. When the lamb has browned, move the pan to the boiling plate, add the flour and Vermouth, stir and bring to the boil, then add the chopped mushrooms.

4 Cover and put in the simmering oven for at least 30 minutes or up to 4 hours.

5 Return the pan to the hot plate or floor of the roasting oven to reduce the juices and serve.

banana tatin

To serve more people: Double the ingredients will fill the 28cms Aga sauté pan and will feed up to 12, in smallish portions

Serves 4 – 6

3 bananas

2 tbsp golden syrup

1 oz (25g) butter

Sponge:

2 eggs

4 oz (110g) self raising flour

4 oz (110g) *butter – if there is time set this beside the Aga for a while to soften to make it easier to mix*

4 oz (110g) dark brown sugar

Oven:

Roasting oven, 200C, 400F, Gas 6

Prepare in advance:

Prepared, unbaked, tatin will keep in the fridge for 24 hours before cooking

Prepare ahead:

Will keep in the fridge for up to 24 hours, reheat in the simmering oven for 20 minutes

Freeze:

No, the bananas go soggy!

1 Tip the golden syrup and butter into the base of a 9" frying pan or heavy, solid based tin and set it onto the simmering plate to melt.

2 Peel and slice the bananas onto the caramel base.

3 For the sponge, mix together the ingredients and spread this over the bananas.

4 Put the grid shelf onto the floor of the roasting oven and set the pan onto it. Bake for about 15 – 20 minutes until the sponge is puffed up and golden.

5 Take the tatin from the oven, leave to cool for five minutes then invert it onto a plate and serve with crème fraîche.

instant ice cream
with no cream

Using bananas with the frozen fruits give a really creamy texture. If you just whizz the mixed fruit without a banana, it will be more of a sorbet.

To feed more people: More bananas and more frozen fruit will feed more people

Serves 4

2 bananas

1 bag (500g) frozen mixed summer fruits

Oven:

None!

Prepare in advance:

Keeps in the freezer for several weeks

Freeze:

Er, yes

1   Peel the bananas and put them into the freezer for an hour or two.

2   Tip the contents of the bag of fruit and the frozen bananas into a processor and whizz to a paste.

3   Eat at once or re-freeze until needed.

Alternatives:

* Use a bag of mixed autumn fruits with the bananas

* Use single fruits, eg. raspberries or blueberries with the bananas

blackberry and
apple crumble

To feed more people: Double the mixture will fill the large roasting tin and will give up to 15 portions

Serves 6

2 lb (900g) cooking apples

1 lb (450g) blackberries

2 tbsp caster sugar

Crumble:

8 oz (225g) wholemeal plain flour

2 oz (55g) porridge oats

4 oz (110g) butter

2 tbsp demerara sugar

Oven:

Baking oven, 180C, 375F, Gas 5

Prepare in advance:

Assembled crumble will keep in the fridge for 24 hours before baking

Prepare ahead:

Will keep warm in the simmering or warming oven for up to an hour

Freeze:

Yes, assembled and ready to bake

1   Core and quarter the apples and cut into slices. Mix with the blackberries and sugar, then tip into an ovenproof dish.

2   Whizz together the flour, oats and butter with one spoonful of the demerara, and spread this over the top of the apples and blackberries.

3   Sprinkle the remaining sugar over the top of the crumble and bake.

4   3, 4 and 5 oven Aga: Slide the grid shelf onto the 4th runners in the baking oven and set the dish onto it. Bake for about 40 minutes until golden brown and bubbling.

5   2 oven Aga: Set the grid shelf on the floor of the roasting oven and set the dish onto it. Slide the plain shelf onto the 3rd runners and bake the crumble for about 30 minutes until golden and bubbling, then transfer to the simmering oven for a further 15 minutes to finish off.

Alternatives:

• Leave out the blackberries and add some mixed dried fruit instead

• Leave out the blackberries and add 4 oz (110g) ready to eat dried apricots

• Use a bag of defrosted frozen mixed fruits – either a summer mix or an apple mix

creamy apple and treacle tart

To feed more people: Double the ingredients will fill a 12" tart case and cut into 12 slices

Serves 4

Pastry:

6 oz (175g) plain flour

3 oz (75g) butter

Grated rind of a lemon

2 tbsp lemon juice

Filling:

1 egg

4 tbsp natural yogurt

6 oz (175g) golden syrup

1 dessert apple

2 slices white bread

Rest of the juice from the lemon

Oven:

Floor of roasting oven

Prepare in advance:

Will keep in the fridge for 24 hours

Prepare ahead:

Will keep warm in simmering or warming oven for an hour

Freeze:

Yes

1   To make the pastry, put the flour, butter and lemon rind into a processor and whizz until the texture of breadcrumbs. With the motor running, add the lemon juice a teaspoon at a time until it comes together as a dough.

2   Roll out the pastry and line a 9"/23cm flan dish. Chill (or freeze) until required.

3   Quarter and core the apple, then put all the filling ingredients into a processor and whizz to a paste.

4   Pour the filling into the prepared case and put it onto the floor of the roasting oven to bake for about 25 minutes until the pastry has browned.

5   The filling will firm up as the tart cools.

gooseberry tart

To feed more people: Double the ingredients will fill a 12"/30cms tin and will cut into 12 pieces

Serves 4 – 6

Pastry:

6 oz plain flour

3 oz butter

½ tsp vanilla extract

2–3 tbsp water

Filling:

1 tub (200g) mascarpone

3 eggs

2 oz (55g) caster sugar

1 tbsp elderflower cordial

12 oz (375g) gooseberries

Oven:

Roasting oven, 200C, 400F, Gas 6

Prepare in advance:

Cooked, cooled tart will keep in the fridge for up to 24 hours

Prepare ahead:

Will keep warm in the simmering or warming oven for up to an hour, or cool slowly beside the Aga

Freeze:

Yes

1 Set the tub of mascarpone onto the back of the Aga to soften.

2 To make the pastry, put the flour, butter and ginger into a processor and whizz until the texture of breadcrumbs. With the motor running, add the water a teaspoon at a time until it comes together as a dough.

3 Roll out the pastry and line a 9"/23cm flan dish. Chill (or freeze) until required.

4 For the filling, tip the gooseberries into the prepared pastry case.

5 Mix together the warm mascarpone, eggs, sugar and elderflower cordial and pour this over the gooseberries.

6 Set the tart onto the floor of the roasting oven for 25 minutes until set and golden.

toffee and date tart

To feed more people: Double the ingredients will fill a 12"/30cms tin and will cut into 12 pieces

Serves 4 – 6

Pastry:

6 oz (175g) plain flour

3 oz (85g) butter

1 tbsp dark brown sugar

¼ tsp vanilla extract

2–3 tbsp water

Filling:

9 oz (250g) chopped dates

7 fl oz (200ml) milk

2 oz (55g) butter

3 oz (85g) plain flour

1 tsp bicarbonate of soda

2 oz (55g) ground almonds

2 eggs

4 oz (110g) dark brown sugar

2 tbsp maple syrup

Oven:

Floor of roasting oven, 200C, 400F, Gas 6

Prepare in advance:

Cooked, cooled tart will keep in the fridge for up to 24 hours

Prepare ahead:

Will keep warm in the simmering or warming oven for up to an hour, or cool slowly beside the Aga

Freeze:

Yes

1   To make the pastry, put the flour, butter, sugar and vanilla into a processor and whizz until the texture of breadcrumbs. With the motor running, add the water a teaspoon at a time until it comes together as a dough.

2   Roll out the pastry and line a 9"/23cm flan dish. Chill (or freeze) until required.

3   For the filling, put the dates, butter and milk into a pan and bring to the boil on the simmering plate. Remove from the heat and leave to cool.

4   Mix together the dates, flour, bicarbonate, almonds, eggs, sugar and syrup.

5   Pour the filling into the pastry case and put onto the floor of the roasting oven for 25 minutes until set and golden.

6   Serve with ice cream and sticky toffee sauce.

pineapple and
coconut tart

To feed more people: Double the ingredients will fill a 12"/30cms tin and will cut into 12 pieces

Serves 6

Pastry:

6 oz (175g) plain flour

3 oz (75g) butter

1 oz (25g) caster sugar

1 egg yolk

2 tbsp cold water

½ tsp ground ginger

Filling:

1 ripe pineapple

1 sachet coconut cream

1 tub (250g) cream cheese

2 eggs

3 oz (75g) caster sugar

1 oz (25g) flaked almonds

Oven:

Roasting oven, 200C, 400F, Gas 6

Prepare ahead:

Will keep in the fridge for up to 24 hours

Freeze:

Yes, especially the uncooked, empty pastry case

1 To make the pastry, put the flour, sugar, butter, ginger and egg yolk into a processor and whizz to the consistency of breadcrumbs. With the motor running, add the water a little at a time, until it forms a dough. Roll out and line a 9" (23cm) ceramic flan dish. Refrigerate until needed.

2 Put the tub of cream cheese onto the back of the Aga to soften. Put the sachet of coconut cream onto the back of the Aga to soften.

3 To assemble the tart, peel, core and slice the pineapple and arrange the slices in the pastry case.

4 Squeeze the sachet of soft coconut cream into a bowl, then add the eggs, cream cheese and sugar. Mix well, then pour over the pineapple base, scatter on the flaked almonds and set onto the floor of the roasting oven. Bake for about 25 minutes, until the pastry is brown and the top risen a little and golden.

5 Dust with icing sugar and serve tepid.

apple mousse

To feed more people: Double the ingredients will fill 10 ramekins for individual portions

Serves 4

2lb (900g) Cox apples

1 oz (25g) butter

3 tbsp water

1 tsp vanilla extract

3 fl oz (60g) honey

½ pint (300ml) double cream

2 tsp gelatine powder

Oven:

Simmering oven, 130C, 250F, Gas 1

Prepare in advance:

Will keep in the fridge for 24 hours

Freeze:

Yes

1   Put the jar of honey onto the back of the Aga to warm up, it is much easier to measure it when it is slightly runny.

2   Peel, core and chop the apples.

3   Put the water into a bowl and sprinkle over the gelatine. Leave this on the back of the Aga for the gelatine to dissolve in the water.

4   Melt the butter in a heavy pan on the simmering plate and tip in the apples and the honey. Put a lid onto the pan and when the lid is too hot to leave your hand on, there is enough steam in the pan to cook the apples. Transfer the pan to the simmering oven for at least 20 minutes, or up to an hour or so.

5   When the apples are soft, stir in the melted gelatine and vanilla extract. Test for sweetness, add a little more honey if necessary. Leave to cool.

6   Whip the cream and fold it into the cooled apples. Pour into individual dishes or a large bowl and chill for a couple of hours before serving.

Ring the changes:

• Use pears instead of apples

• Add some blackberries or raspberries in season

strawberry and
rose pudding

Serves 4 – 6

1 lb (450g) strawberries

4 oz (110g) caster sugar

4 oz (110g) butter

2 eggs

1 tbsp rosewater

6 oz (175g) self raising flour

Oven:

Roasting oven 200C, 400F, Gas 6,
and simmering oven, 130C, 250F,
Gas 1

Prepare in advance:

Roast the strawberries in advance
but the pudding is nicest eaten on
the day it is made

Prepare ahead:

Leave in simmering or warming
oven for another hour if necessary

Freeze:

*Cooked, cooled pudding will
freeze in its pudding bowl. Defrost
and put the pudding, still sealed in
its bowl, into the simmering oven
for an hour to warm up*

If you cannot find rosewater, orange flower water
makes an interesting change

1 Set the butter in a bowl beside the Aga to soften. Hull
and halve the strawberries.

2 Line a small roasting tin with Bake-O-Glide and tip
the strawberries into it.

3 Hang the tin from the 4th runners in the roasting oven
for about 10 minutes, until the strawberries are
softened and bubbling.

4 Line a 2 pint / 1 litre pudding basin with cling film. Put
about half of the roasted strawberries into the bowl,
with one teaspoon of the rosewater.

5 Beat together the butter, sugar, eggs, flour and
vanilla. Stir in the remaining strawberries and
rosewater.

6 Tip this mixture into the prepared bowl and cover with
cling film.

7 Put about an inch / 2.5cms of water into a large pan,
put in the bowl and put on the lid. Bring to the boil on
the boiling plate, and transfer the whole thing to the
simmering oven for at least 2 hours, up to 4 hours if
necessary.

8 To serve, remove from the pan, take off the cling film
lid and upend onto a plate. The strawberries in the
bottom of the bowl will cascade down the sides of
the pudding.

9 Serve with custard (and cream!)

Alternatives:

- Serve the roasted strawberries and rosewater with yogurt or cream to make strawberry
fool
- Mix the roasted strawberries and rosewater with a couple of eggs and a tub of crème
fraîche into a pastry case to bake as a tart

rhubarb gingerbread

Is it a cake? Is it a pudding? Both!

To feed more people: Double the ingredients will fill the small roasting tin

Serves 6

5 oz (150g) salted butter

4 oz (110g) dark brown sugar

6 oz (175g) golden syrup

3 oz (85g) black treacle

1 tsp ground ginger

1 tsp ground allspice

10 oz (300g) wholemeal self raising flour

1 tsp bicarbonate of soda

2 eggs

12 oz (375g) fresh rhubarb

Oven:

Baking oven, 170C, 350F, Gas 4

Prepare in advance:

Cake keeps in a tin or the fridge for 36 hours

Prepare ahead:

Keep warm in the simmering or warming oven for an hour

Freeze:

Yes

1 Set the butter in a bowl on the back of the Aga to soften. Set the tins of syrup and treacle onto the back of the Aga to warm up. Boil the kettle.

2 Line an 8″ / 20cms square tin with Bake-O-Glide.

3 Cut the rhubarb into 1″/2 ½cms pieces.

4 Beat the butter and sugar together, then add the syrup and treacle.

5 Dissolve the bicarbonate of soda in ¼ pint (150ml) boiling water and stir this into the mixture, then add the ginger, allspice, flour and eggs and beat well.

6 Tip the rhubarb into the prepared tin then pour the cake batter over the top and bake.

7 3, 4 and 5 oven Aga: Set the grid shelf onto the floor of the baking oven and bake the cake for about 45 – 60 minutes until it is set and golden.

8 2 oven Aga: Set the tin into the large roasting tin and hang this from the 4th lowest, runners in the roasting oven. Slide the cold plain shelf onto the 2nd runners above. After about half an hour, move the roasting tin and its contents to the simmering oven and bake for a further 30 to 45 minutes until set and golden.

9 Turn the cake out and eat it warm as a pudding or cold as a cake.

Alternatives:

• Use chopped cooking apples instead of the rhubarb

• Use gooseberries instead of the rhubarb

chocolate bombe

To feed more people: Double the ingredients will fill at 4 pint / 2 litre bowl and will serve up to 12

Serves 4 – 6

½ pint (300ml) double cream

3 oz (85g) white chocolate

8 oz (225g) plain chocolate

4 eggs

2 tbsp brandy or strong black coffee (both optional)

Oven:

Back of Aga to melt the chocolate

Prepare ahead:

Will keep in the fridge for up to 24 hours

Freeze:

Yes, serve as a serious iced chocolate pudding or defrost and eat cold

1   Set the two types of chocolate into separate bowls on the back of the Aga to melt.

2   Line a 2 pint (1 litre) pudding basin with cling film.

3   Whip the cream and stir in the melted white chocolate. Spread this over the base and up the sides of the prepared pudding basin and put this into the freezer to set.

4   Separate the eggs. Stir the egg yolks and brandy into the melted dark chocolate.

5   Whisk the egg whites until they stand in peaks, then fold into the chocolate. Pour into the cream lined bowl and chill for a couple of hours. It is even better the next day.

astonishing strawberries

To feed more people: Double the ingredients will serve up to 10. Three pounds of strawberries and double the sauce will feed up to 15

Serves 4

2 limes

4 oz (110g) caster sugar

½ tsp ground peppercorns

1 lb (450g) strawberries

Oven:

Simmering plate

Prepare in advance:

Will keep in the fridge for 24 hours, but serve at room temperature

Freeze:

No

1   Hull the strawberries and cut them into halves. Put into a wide dish in a single layer.

2   Grate the zest from one lime and put it into a pan, with the squeezed juice of both of the limes, the sugar and pepper. Set the pan onto the simmering plate and heat until the sugar has dissolved.

3   Pour the warm syrup over the strawberries and leave to cool.

4   Serve with really good vanilla ice cream

griese torte

This is a fairly shallow sponge, but useful as it contains no flour and no fat (until you add the cream in the filling!)

To feed more people: Double the ingredients will fill a 10" tin and will cut into 12 smaller slices

Serves 4

3 eggs

4 oz (110g) caster sugar

2 oz (75g) semolina

½ oz (12g) ground almonds

1 lemon

½ pint (300ml) double cream

2 pears

Oven:

Baking oven, 160C, 350F, Gas 4

Prepare in advance:

Will keep in the fridge for 24 hours

Freeze:

Yes, without the pears, try raspberries instead!

1 Line an 8"/20cms round cake tin with Bake-O-Glide.

2 Separate the eggs. Beat the egg yolks with the sugar until it is light and fluffy, then grate the lemon zest into the bowl, squeeze the juice and add that. Whisk this mixture until it is thick.

3 Whisk the egg whites and fold them into the yolk and lemon mixture, then fold in the semolina and ground almonds. Pour the cake mixture into the tin and bake.

4 3, 4 and 5 oven Aga: Set the grid shelf onto the floor of the oven and put the cake tin onto it. Bake for about 20 minutes until golden brown and risen, then transfer to the simmering oven for a further 10 minutes to set completely.

5 2 oven Aga: set the cake tin into the large roasting tin and hang this from the 4th, lowest, runners in the roasting oven. Slide the cold plain shelf onto the second runners above. Bake the cake for about 15 minutes until it has risen and the top is beginning to brown, then transfer the roasting tin and its contents to the simmering oven for about 25 minutes until the cake is cooked. Don't forget to remove the plain shelf from the roasting oven!

6 Take the cooked cake from the oven and allow to cool in the tin for 5 minutes before turning out onto a cooling rack.

7 Whip the cream until it is thick.

8 Split the cooled cake into two layers and spread the cream over the bottom layer, slice the pears and lay them on top, then put the top layer of the cake on top. Dust with icing sugar and serve.

strawberry and
orange pavlova

Serves 8

4 egg whites

8 oz (225g) caster sugar

2 oranges

2 oz (55g) caster sugar

½ pint (284ml pot) double cream

1 tub (250g) mascarpone

1 pack (100g) white chocolate drops

Oven:

Simmering oven, 130C, 250F, Gas 1 or warming oven, 85C, 150F, Gas 1/4

Prepare ahead:

Meringue will keep in an airtight tin for a week, or freeze it. Filling will keep for 24 hours in the fridge, assemble an hour or less before serving

Freeze:

Yes

1 First, make the pavlova: Whisk the egg whites until stiff then, continuing to whisk, add the sugar a spoonful at a time.

2 Spread the meringue mix over a piece of Bake-O-Glide into a fairly neat circle, with the edges slightly higher than the centre.

3 4 and 5 oven Aga: Put the meringue, on the plain shelf, into the warming oven for about 48 hours.

4 2 and 3 oven Aga: Hang the plain shelf from the 4th, lowest runners in the simmering oven and bake for about an hour or an hour and a half. Transfer the shelf to the top of the Aga and set it onto the closed lids overnight, to continue drying out.

5 For the filling: Grate the rind and squeeze the juice from the oranges. Set the mascarpone in its tub on the back of the Aga to soften. Tip the white chocolate into a bowl and set onto the back of the Aga to melt.

6 Whip the cream until it is thick, then fold in the mascarpone, sugar, melted white chocolate and the orange juice and rind.

7 Pile into the centre of the cooled meringue and scatter the strawberries on top, then chill and serve within an hour or two.

lemon and lime pavlova

Serves 8

4 egg whites

8 oz (225g) caster sugar

1 lemon

1 lime

6 oz (175g) caster sugar

½ pint (284ml pot) double cream

1 tub (250g) mascarpone

1 lime

Oven:

Simmering oven, 130C, 250F,
Gas 1 or warming oven, 85C, 150F,
Gas 1/4

Prepare in advance:

Will keep for 48 hours in the fridge

Freeze:

Yes

1 First, make the pavlova: Whisk the egg whites until stiff then, continuing to whisk, add the sugar a spoonful at a time.

2 Spread the meringue mix over a piece of Bake-O-Glide into a fairly neat circle, with the edges slightly higher than the centre.

3 4 and 5 oven Aga: Put the meringue, on the plain shelf, into the warming oven for about 48 hours.

4 2 and 3 oven Aga: Hang the plain shelf from the 4th, lowest runners in the simmering oven and bake for about an hour or an hour and a half. Transfer the shelf to the top of the Aga and set it onto the closed lids overnight, to continue drying out.

5 For the filling: Grate the rind and squeeze the juice from the lemon and lime. Set the mascarpone in its tub on the back of the Aga to soften.

6 Put the cream and sugar into a pan and heat gently on the simmering plate until the sugar has dissolved and the cream is not quite boiling.

7 Beat the mascarpone into the hot cream, then beat in the lemon and lime juice and rind. Leave to cool.

8 Pour into the centre of the cooled meringue and grate the rind of another lime on top, then chill for a couple of hours.

9 Serve with a big bowl of strawberries.

pear and ginger brioche pudding

To feed more people: Double the ingredients will fill the large roasting tin and will feed 8 greedy people or 12 people who are full after a large main course

Serves 4

½ oz (10g) butter

4 large ripe pears

1 tin condensed caramel

¾ pint (450ml) milk

2 balls of stem ginger from a jar and 1 tbsp of the syrup

3 eggs

1 brioche loaf

4 oz (100g) sultanas

2 tbsp demerara sugar

Oven:

Baking oven, 180C, 375F, Gas 5

Prepare in advance:

Uncooked, assembled pudding will keep in the fridge for up to 24 hours

Prepare ahead:

Will keep warm in the simmering or warming oven for an hour

Freeze:

No, the custard will separate when reheated

1 Set the butter onto the back of the Aga to melt. Brush an Aga Portmeirion deep baking dish with the butter or line the small deep roasting tin with Bake-O-Glide.

2 Peel, core and quarter the pears and cut them into slices. Slice the brioche loaf. Grate the stem ginger.

3 Beat the eggs and milk together in a jug and stir in the ginger and syrup. Mix in the caramel.

4 Lay slices of the brioche into the dish. Add a layer of pears and half of the sultanas, then another layer of brioche, another layer of pears and finish with a final layer of brioche.

5 Pour the egg and milk mixture over the pudding and leave to soak for half an hour, or overnight.

6 Scatter the demerara sugar over the top of the pudding and bake.

7 <u>3, 4 and 5 oven Aga:</u> Hang the dish from the 3rd runners in the baking oven.

8 <u>2 oven Aga:</u> Set the dish into the large roasting tin and hang the tin from the 4th, lowest runners in the roasting oven. Slide the cold shelf onto the 2nd runners above.

9 Bake the pudding for about half an hour, until it is golden and crunchy on top. Serve with a dollop of natural yogurt, or cream.

pear and chocolate puff

To feed more people: Double the ingredients will fill the large roasting tin and will make up to 14 portions

Serves 4 – 6

6 ripe pears

2 packs (200g) chocolate drops – milk, plain or white or a mixture, or maybe some fudge drops

5 oz (150g) plain flour

4 oz (110g) butter

½ pint (300ml) milk

4 eggs

Oven:

Roasting oven, 200C, 400F, Gas 6

Prepare in advance:

The paste will keep in the fridge for 24 hours before using

Prepare ahead:

Will keep warm in the simmering or warming oven for half an hour

Freeze:

Uncooked pudding will freeze, defrost before cooking

1 Put the butter and milk into a pan and set on the simmering plate.

2 When the mixture is boiling, tip in the flour and beat well until it is incorporated into a thick paste. Beat in the eggs one at a time and keep beating until it is a thick and glossy paste. Set aside to cool.

3 Quarter and core the pears and lay them into the small roasting tin or an oven proof dish.

4 Scatter the chocolate drops over the pears.

5 Spoon the milk and egg paste over the top of the pears and chocolate.

6 Hang the tin or dish from the second runners in the roasting oven and bake for about 20–25 minutes until puffed up and golden. *It will puff up more around the edges than in the centre of the dish*.

7 Serve with a spoonful of crème fraîche or natural yogurt.

lemon roulade

To feed more people: Make a second roulade and you should get up to 14 portions

Serves 6

5 eggs

5 oz (150g) caster sugar

2 oz (55g) ground almonds

4 oz (110g) self raising flour

2 lemons

½ pint (275ml) cream

3 tbsp lemon curd

Pack (200g) raspberries

Icing sugar to finish

Oven:

Baking oven, 175C, 350F, Gas 4

Prepare in advance:

Will keep in fridge for up to 24 hours

Freeze:

Yes, wrapped in kitchen paper to absorb any moisture that comes off as it defrosts

1 Line the large roasting tin with Bake-O-Glide.

2 Separate the eggs. Grate the rind from the lemon and squeeze the juice.

3 Whisk the whites until stiff. Whisk the egg yolks and sugar until light and fluffy. Whisk in the grated lemon rind and the juice. Fold the almonds and flour into the mixture, then fold in the egg whites.

4 Pour into the tin, spread evenly and bake.

5 3, 4 and 5 oven Aga: Hang the tin from the lowest runners in the baking oven for about 20 minutes until risen and golden.

6 2 oven Aga: Hang the tin from the lowest runners in the roasting oven and slide the cold shelf onto the second runners for about 15 minutes until risen and golden.

7 Take the cake from the oven and turn it out onto a clean tea towel. Remove the Bake-O-Glide and roll the roulade in the towel and leave to cool.

8 When the roulade is cool, whip the cream and stir in the lemon curd. Spread this over the unrolled roulade, scatter on the raspberries, then re-roll it. Chill for an hour before serving, dusted with icing sugar.

lemon bread and
butter pudding

To feed more people: Double the ingredients will fill the large roasting tin and will divide into 12 portions

Serves 4 – 6

8 slices brioche

1 jar lemon curd

2 eggs

¾ pint (450ml) milk

½ oz (12g) butter

Oven:

Baking oven, 350F, 180C, Gas 4

Prepare in advance:

Assembled, uncooked pudding will keep in the fridge for 24 hours

Prepare ahead:

Will keep warm in the simmering or warming oven for up to an hour

Freeze:

No

1   Spread the lemon curd over the slices of brioche.

2   Grease an Aga Portmeirion baking dish with the butter or line the small roasting tin with Bake-O-Glide, then put in the slices of brioche in layers.

3   Beat the eggs with the milk and remaining lemon curd and pour over the brioche.

4   Leave to stand for half an hour then bake for about 35 minutes, until puffed up and golden brown.

5   3, 4 and 5 oven Aga: Set the grid shelf on the floor of the baking oven and put the dish onto it.

6   2 oven Aga: Set the dish into the large roasting tin and hang it from the 4th runners in the roasting oven. Slide the cold plain shelf onto the 2nd runners above.

7   Serve with cream or crème fraîche or custard. Or all three . . .

christmas cheesecake

To feed more people: Double the ingredients will fill an 11" tin with a deep cheesecake, or a 12" tin with a slightly shallower cheesecake

Serves 4 – 6

9 oz (250g) ginger nut biscuits

3 oz (85g) butter

2 tubs (500g) cream cheese

5 oz (150g) caster sugar

1 tub (300g) crème fraîche

4 eggs

1 orange

1 jar mincemeat

Oven:

Back of Aga, simmering oven,
130C, 250F, Gas 1

Prepare in advance:

Will keep in the fridge for 24 hours

Freeze:

Yes

1 Set the butter in a bowl onto the back of the Aga to melt. Set the tubs of cream cheese onto the back of the Aga to warm up and soften.

2 Line a 9"/23cms loose based tin with Bake-O-Glide.

3 Crush the biscuits and mix with the melted butter and press this mixture into the bottom of the prepared tin. Chill, if time allows.

4 Grate the rind of the orange into a large bowl, and add the cream cheese, sugar and crème fraîche. Mix thoroughly.

5 Stir in the mincemeat, swirling it rather than mixing it in completely. Pour the filling onto the biscuit base in the tin.

6 Bake the cheesecake in the simmering oven for about an hour and a half, the filling will still be slightly wobbly when it comes out, but it will firm up as it cools.

7 Chill for about 4 hours until completely set.

8 To serve, remove the cheesecake from the tin and slide it onto a plate. Shake a little icing sugar over the top to show you have made a festive effort.

lavender cheesecake

To feed more people: Double the ingredients will fill an 11" with a deep cheesecake, or a 12" tin with a slightly shallower cheesecake

Serves 4

9 oz (250g) Amaretti biscuits

4 oz (21210g) butter

½ pint (300ml) double cream

2 tubs (500g) cream cheese

2 oz (55g) caster sugar

1 lemon

7 oz (200g) set natural yogurt

5 sprigs of lavender (or rosemary)

Oven:

Back of Aga, simmering plate

Prepare in advance:

Will keep in the fridge for 24 hours

Freeze:

Yes

1   Set the butter in a bowl onto the back of the Aga to melt. Set the tubs of cream cheese onto the back of the Aga to warm up and soften.

2   Heat the cream, in a heavy pan on the simmering plate, with the sugar and two of the lavender sprigs until almost boiling, then remove from the heat and allow to cool completely.

3   Line a 9"/23cms loose based tin with Bake-O-Glide.

4   Crush the biscuits and mix with the melted butter and press this mixture into the bottom of the prepared tin. Chill, if time allows.

5   Grate the rind of the lemon and add it to the cooled cream, stir in a tablespoonful of the juice. Mix in the softened cream cheese and the yogurt, then pour onto the biscuit base in the tin.

6   Chill for about 4 hours until completely set.

7   To serve, remove the cheesecake from the tin and slide it onto a plate. Lay a couple of sprigs of lavender on top and serve scattered with icing sugar and maybe a couple of crushed lavender flowers.

lime mousse

To feed more people: Make this quantity in a 1 pint/500ml loaf tin, to feed 8. Double the quantity will fill a 10" / 25cms tin or 16 ramekins

Serves 6

2 limes

1 lemon

4 oz (110g) caster sugar

½ tsp cardamom seeds, removed from the pods

3 eggs

½ pint (284 ml) crème fraîche or natural yogurt

1 tbsp powdered gelatine

1 tbsp icing sugar to serve

Oven:

Back of Aga

Prepare in advance:

Finished mousse will keep in fridge for up to 24 hours

Freeze:

Yes

1 Wash and dry the lemon and limes, then grate the rind into a large bowl. Squeeze the juice into a smaller bowl.

2 Sprinkle the gelatine over the juice and leave to stand for a minute, then set the bowl into a pan of simmering water to melt or just leave it on the back of the Aga for an hour.

3 Separate the eggs and put the yolks into the bowl with the lemon rind, together with the sugar and cardamom seeds. Put the egg whites into another large bowl.

4 Whip the egg whites. Then whisk the egg yolks, lemon rind and sugar until thick and pale. *(No need to wash the beaters if you do it in the right order, creating a little less washing up.)*

5 Whisk the juice and gelatine into the yolk mixture, leave to cool for a few minutes then fold in the crème fraîche or yogurt and whisked whites. Pour into 6 ramekins or one pretty glass bowl and chill until needed.

6 Serve with some icing sugar sifted over the top to show that you have made an effort.

green scones

Makes about 30 tiny ones, or 15 if using a 2" cutter

4 oz (110g) frozen spinach

9 oz (250g) self raising flour

2 oz (55g) butter

½ tsp baking powder

1 egg

2 fl oz (55ml) milk

Beaten egg to glaze

Grated nutmeg

Salt and pepper

Filling:

7 oz (200g) pack garlic and herb cheese

Oven:

Roasting oven, 200C, 400F, Gas 6

Prepare ahead:

3 hours

Freeze:

Yes, unfilled

1   Whizz together all scone ingredients. Knead gently on a board then roll out until ½"/1cm thick.

2   Using a 1"2½cm cutter, cut into rounds.

3   Line the cold plan shelf with Bake-O-Glide.

4   Put the scones onto the shelf and brush with beaten egg.

5   Slide the shelf into the roasting oven on the 2nd runners. Bake for 6–8 minutes.

6   When the scones have cooled, split and fill with the cheese.

7   Sandwich together and serve.

american corn muffins

To feed more people: Double the quantity will make 24 muffins. Cook them in smaller bun tins to make 18 from this mixture

Makes 12

6 oz (175g) plain flour

6 oz (175g) cornmeal or polenta

2 tsp bicarbonate of soda

½ tsp baking powder

1 tsp salt

1 tsp caster sugar

2 oz (55g) butter

8 fl oz (250ml) buttermilk or skimmed milk

2 oz (55g) Cheddar cheese

2 eggs

Oven:

Roasting oven, 200C, 400F, Gas 6

Prepare in advance:

Will keep in a tin for 48 hours

Freeze:

Yes

1   Set the butter in a bowl on the back of the Aga to melt.

2   Line the holes of a 12 hole muffin tin with paper cases, or grease each hole thoroughly.

3   Put all the ingredients into a processor and whiz to mix, or just mix everything together in a bowl.

4   Pour the mixture into the muffin tin.

5   Set the grid shelf onto the floor of the roasting oven and put the muffin tin onto it.

6   Bake for about 10–12 minutes until puffed up and golden.

Spice it up a bit: Add a couple of chopped green chillies to the mixture or some dried chipotle chillies

cheese and
pepper muffins

Makes 12, or about 30 mini muffins

1 medium courgette

6 peppadew peppers

3 oz (85g) Cheddar cheese

4 oz (110g) camembert

1 tsp mixed dried *fines herbes*

9 oz (250g) self raising flour

1 tsp baking powder

2 eggs

4 oz (120ml) milk

5 tbsp rapeseed oil

Oven:

Baking oven, 180C, 375F, Gas 5

Prepare in advance:

Will keep in a tin for a day

Freeze:

Yes

1 Grate the courgette and chop the peppadew peppers.

2 Grate the Cheddar and cut the camembert into small cubes.

3 Mix together the flour, herbs, baking powder, eggs, milk and oil. Add the courgette, peppers and cheeses.

4 Line a 12–hole muffin tin with paper cases.

5 Divide the mixture between the cases and bake.

6 3, 4 and 5 oven Aga: Slide the grid shelf onto the 2nd runners in the baking oven and put the tin onto it. Bake the muffins for about 25 minutes.

7 2 oven Aga: Set the grid shelf on the floor of the roasting oven and put the tin onto it. Slide the cold plain shelf onto the 3rd runners and bake the muffins for about 20–25 minutes.

banana and lemon loaf

To feed more people: Double the ingredients will fill a 8" square tin and will cut into many squares

Serves 4 – 6

2 eggs

4 oz (110g) soft brown sugar

4 oz (110g) butter

2 bananas

8 oz (225g) self raising wholemeal flour

2 tbsp lemon curd

½ tsp ground allspice

Oven:

Baking oven, 160C, 350F, Gas 4

Prepare in advance:

Will keep in a tin for two or three days

Freeze:

Yes

1 Line a 2lb loaf tin with Bake-O-Glide. If possible, set the butter beside the Aga to soften for half an hour before making the cake.

2 Peel and mash the bananas. Beat in the rest of the ingredients and pour into the prepared tin and bake.

3 3, 4 and 5 oven Aga: Set the grid shelf onto the floor of the oven and put the loaf tin onto it. Bake for about 40 minutes until golden brown and risen.

4 2 oven Aga: set the cake tin into the large roasting tin and hang this from the 4th, lowest, runners in the roasting oven. Slide the cold plain shelf onto the second runners above. Bake the loaf for about 25 minutes until it has risen and the top is beginning to brown, then transfer the roasting tin and its contents to the simmering oven for a further 35 minutes until the loaf is cooked. Don't forget to remove the plain shelf from the roasting oven!

5 Take the cooked loaf from the oven and allow to cool in the tin for 5 minutes before turning out onto a cooling rack.

6 Serve in slices.

banana and chocolate with extra chocolate cake

To feed more people: Double the quantity will fill the large roasting tin and should cut into 48 squares

Makes 24 pieces

3 x 100g packs white chocolate drops

9 oz (250g) butter

5 eggs

2 large bananas

5 oz (150g) wholemeal self raising flour

4 oz (110g) cocoa powder

12 oz (375g) light soft brown sugar

Oven:

Baking oven, 180C, 375F, Gas 5

Prepare in advance:

These improve with keeping for a day or two in a well-hidden tin

Freeze:

Yes

1 Put the butter in a bowl on the back of the Aga to melt. Tip one of the bags of chocolate drops into a bowl and set it on the back of the Aga to melt.

2 Line the small roasting tin with Bake-O-Glide.

3 Peel the bananas and mash in a bowl, then add the rest of the ingredients except the melted white chocolate. Mix well and pour into the tin.

4 3, 4 and 5 oven Aga: Hang the tin from the 2nd runners in the baking oven and bake for about 40–45 minutes until just set but slightly wobbly in the centre.

5 2 oven Aga: Put the tin into the large roasting tin and hang this from the 4th runners in the roasting oven. Slide the cold plain shelf 2 runners above. Bake for about 35 minutes until just set.

6 Take the baked cake from the oven and leave to cool in the tin, then turn out onto a cooling rack.

7 To serve, mix the melted white chocolate with the icing sugar and spread it over the top of the cake and cut into 24 squares.

chocolate chunk cookies

To feed more people: Double the ingredients will make a lot more cookies – especially if you roll the dough into a longer, thinner log shape

Serves 4

12 oz (350g) plain flour

1 tsp bicarbonate of soda

8 oz (225g) butter

6 oz (175g) caster sugar

6 oz (175g) light muscovado sugar

1 tsp vanilla extract

½ tsp salt

2 eggs

12 oz (350g) chocolate chips

Oven:

Baking oven, 190C, 375F, Gas 5

Prepare in advance:

Wrapped dough will keep in the fridge for 48 hours

Prepare ahead:

Eat as soon as they are cold enough to handle!

Freeze:

Wrapped dough freezes really well, slide and bake from frozen

1   Put all the ingredients except the chocolate into a processor and whizz to a dough. Or mix by hand.

2   Mix in the chocolate.

3   Shape into two logs and wrap in clingfilm, chill or freeze until needed.

4   Slice into ¼" rounds and lay on the plain shelf, covered with Bake-O-Glide.

5   <u>3, 4 and 5 oven Aga:</u> Slide the shelf onto the top runners in the baking oven and bake for about 10 minutes.

6   <u>2 oven Aga:</u> Put the grid shelf onto the floor of the roasting oven. Slide the shelf of cookies onto it and bake for 8 minutes.

7   Leave to cool and firm up on the shelf before transferring to a cooling rack and watch them vanish.

Aga tip: 'Bake stable' chocolate chips are designed not to melt as they get hot, so they keep their shape as they cook

millionaire's
shortbread

To feed more people: Double the ingredients will fill the large roasting tin and will cut into 48 squares

Makes 24 smallish squares

12 oz (375g) self raising flour

1 packet (250g) salted butter

4 oz (110g) caster sugar

1 tin (340g) Carnation caramel

7 oz (200g) plain chocolate

Oven:

Baking oven, 160C, 350F, Gas 4

Prepare in advance:

Will keep in a well hidden tin for
several days

Freeze:

Yes

1   Line the small roasting tin with Bake-O-Glide.

2   Put the chocolate in a bowl on the back of the Aga to melt. Set the tin of caramel onto the back of the Aga to warm up and soften.

3   Whizz the sugar, butter and flour in a processor until it sticks together as a crumbly dough.

4   Tip the dough into the tin and press down firmly.

5   3, 4 and 5 oven Aga: Hang the tin from the 4th runners in the baking oven and bake for about 20 minutes until pale golden.

6   2 oven Aga: Set the tin into the large roasting tin and hang this from the 4th runners in the roasting oven. Slide the cold plain shelf onto the 2nd runners above and bake for about 15 minutes until pale golden.

7   Leave the shortbread in the tin until it is completely cold and set firm.

8   Turn the shortbread out of the tin and put onto a plate.

9   Spread the warm caramel over the shortbread, then pour the melted chocolate onto the caramel and spread to the edges.

10 Leave to cool until the chocolate has set before cutting into squares.

pear and
flapjack pie

To feed more people: Double the ingredients will make a pie in the large shallow baking tray, but beware of the pastry cooking too fast on the floor of the oven, move it to the 4th runners after 10 minutes

Serves 6

For the pastry:

8 oz (225g) plain flour

4 oz (110g) butter

1 tbsp caster sugar

½ tsp ground cinnamon

2 – 3 tbsp water

For the filling:

2 pears

4 oz (110g) butter

4 oz (110g) demerara sugar

2 tbsp golden syrup

6 oz (175g) porridge oats

Oven:

Roasting oven, 195C, 375F, Gas 5

Prepare ahead:

Pie will keep in an airtight tin for up to 3 days, if no one finds them first

Freeze:

Yes

1. To make the pastry, put the flour, butter, sugar and cinnamon into a processor and whizz until the texture of breadcrumbs. With the motor running, add the water a teaspoon at a time until it comes together as a dough.

2. Roll out the pastry and line the shallow Portmeirion baking tray or a ceramic dish 12″ x 8″ (30 x 20cms). Chill (or freeze) until required.

3. Put the butter, sugar and golden syrup into a pan and set on the simmering plate to melt together.

4. Slice the pears into very thin slices.

5. When the butter mixture has melted, stir in the oats.

6. Spread the pears over the pastry, then tip the flapjack mixture over the pears and smooth the top.

7. Set the dish onto the floor of the roasting oven and slide the cold plain shelf onto the 3rd runners and bake for about 20 minutes until golden.

8. Serve the pie from the dish, with custard or cream or crème fraîche or all three!

To speed up the process, use a sheet of ready-made shortcrust pastry and add the cinnamon to the pears instead of making the pastry

chocolate and
ginger bake

No eggs in this cake, which makes it really useful for anyone with egg allergies

To feed more people: Double all of the ingredients will fill the large roasting tin and will cut into about 40 pieces

Makes 16 pieces

5 oz (150g) butter

4 oz (110g) dark brown sugar

7 oz (200g) golden syrup

7 oz (200g) black treacle

1 tsp ground ginger

1 tsp ground allspice

4 oz (110g) plain chocolate

7 fl oz (200ml) milk

11 oz (300g) plain flour

1 tsp bicarbonate of soda

Icing:

5 oz (150g) icing sugar

1 tbsp black treacle

2 oz (55g) butter

Oven:

Baking oven, 180C, 375F, Gas 4

Prepare in advance:

This cake improves on keeping!

Hide it in a tin for a few days

Freeze:

Yes

1   To measure the treacle and syrup, set the tins or jars onto the back of the Aga to warm up, which will make them easier to pour into the pan when it is on the scales.

2   Line the small roasting tin with Bake-O-Glide.

3   Measure the butter, sugar, syrup, treacle, spices and chocolate into a pan and set it on the back of the Aga for an hour to melt. OR heat the pan very gently on the simmering plate until everything has melted but not boiled, since this will separate the chocolate.

4   Stir the milk and bicarbonate of soda into the pan, then fold in the flour.

5   Pour the mixture into the prepared tin and bake for about 35 minutes.

6   <u>3, 4 and 5 oven Aga:</u> Hang the tin from the 3rd runners in the baking oven.

7   <u>2 oven Aga:</u> Set the small roasting tin onto the large roasting tin and slide this onto the 4th runners in the roasting oven, with the plain shelf on the 2nd runners above.

8   Take the cake from the oven when it is cooked and allow to cool in the tin.

9   For the icing: Set the butter and treacle in a bowl on the back of the Aga to melt. Stir in the icing sugar and spread over the cake.

white chocolate and raspberry traybake

Serves up to 8 as a pudding, more if cut into squares for tea

To feed more people: Double the ingredients will bake in the large roasting tin and cut into about 30 pieces

7 oz (200g) butter

4 oz (110g) white chocolate

4 eggs

6 oz (175g) light muscovado sugar

7 oz (200g) self raising flour

6 oz (175g) raspberries

Topping:

4 oz (110g) white chocolate

1 pack (200g) cream cheese

3 oz (85g) icing sugar

Oven:

Baking oven, 175C, 350F, Gas 4

Prepare in advance:

Cake keeps well in the fridge for 24 hours

Freeze:

Yes

1 Set the butter and white chocolate in a bowl onto the back of the Aga to melt for half an hour. Go and have a cup of coffee or something while it melts.

2 Line the small roasting tin with Bake-O-Glide.

3 Beat the eggs, sugar and flour into the melted butter and chocolate mixture, then fold in all but a few of the raspberries.

4 Bake the cake for about 25 minutes.

5 3, 4 and 5 oven Aga: Hang the tin from the 3rd runners in the baking oven.

6 2 oven Aga: Set the small tin into the large roasting tin and hang this from the 4th, lowest runners in the roasting oven. Slide the cold plain shelf onto the 2nd runners above.

7 While the cake is baking, set the pack of cream cheese and the bowl of white chocolate onto the back of the Aga to soften.

8 Cool the baked cake, then mix together the white chocolate and cream cheese, stir in the icing sugar and spread the mixture over the cake. Decorate with a few raspberries if you have not put them all into the cake mix!

Aga tip: The raspberries can be fresh or frozen – if using still frozen fruit, it will take an extra 5 minutes to defrost and bake in the cake

Aga tip: Be careful to avoid 'bake stable' white chocolate drops, they won't melt!

chunky brownies

To feed more people: Double the mixture will fill the small roasting tin and make 24 brownies

Makes 12

6 oz (175g) plain chocolate

6 oz (175g) butter

3 eggs

8 oz (225g) caster sugar

½ tsp vanilla extract

4 oz (110g) plain flour

½ tsp salt

3 oz (85g) chopped pecan nuts or dried cranberries

Oven:

Baking oven, 180C, 350F, Gas 4

Prepare in advance:

Bake as soon as mixed

Prepare ahead:

Will improve if kept in a well-hidden tin for a day or two

Freeze:

Yes

1 Line an 8"/20cms tin with Bake-O-Glide.

2 Put the butter and chocolate into a bowl on the back of the Aga to melt.

3 Mix together the eggs, sugar, vanilla and stir into the melted chocolate and butter, then beat in the nuts or fruit, flour and salt.

4 Pour the mixture into the prepared tin and bake.

5 3, 4 and 5 oven Aga: Set the tin onto the grid shelf on the floor of the baking oven and bake for 20 – 22 minutes until just set.

6 2 oven Aga: Set the tin into the large toasting tin and hang this from the 4th, lowest runners in the roasting oven. Slide the cold plain shelf onto the 2nd runners above. Bake for about 18 – 20 minutes until just set.

7 Leave the brownies in the tin to cool before turning out onto a rack to become completely cold. Cut into squares and dust with icing sugar.

profiteroles or éclairs

Makes up to 20

¼ pint (150ml) water

2 oz (55g) butter

2½ oz (65g) plain flour

2 eggs

Oven:

Roasting oven, 200C, 400F, Gas 6

Prepare in advance:

Mix together the choux pastry and keep in the fridge for up to 24 hours

Prepare ahead:

Will keep in a tin, unfilled, for a day or two

Freeze:

Yes, defrost and reheat in the roasting oven for 5 minutes only

1 Put the cold plain shelf into the roasting oven to heat up.

2 Put the water and butter into a heavy based pan and slowly bring to the boil on the simmering plate. When it is boiling, tip in the flour and beat well. Off the heat, break in the eggs one at a time and beat well.

3 Lay a sheet of Bake-O-Glide on the work surface and then either pipe or spoon blobs of the mixture onto the sheet.

4 Take the now hot shelf from the oven and slide on the Bake-O-Glide. Hang the shelf from the third set of runners and bake for 15 minutes until the pastry is golden and puffed up.

5 Fill the pastry puffs with whipped cream and dip them in chocolate before serving.

pecan nut meringue biscuits

To feed more people: Double the mixture will make up to 50 smaller biscuits

Makes about 20

3 oz (85g) pecan nuts

2 oz (55g) plain flour

6 oz (175g) caster sugar

2 egg whites

Oven:

Roasting oven, 200C, 400F, Gas 6

Prepare in advance:

Biscuits will keep in a well-hidden airtight tin for a week or so

Freeze:

Yes

1 Grind the nuts to a powder in a processor.

2 Add the flour and sugar to the nuts and whizz to mix.

3 Whisk the whites until thick, then fold in the nut, flour and sugar mixture.

4 Line the plain shelf with Bake-O-Glide and drop spoonsful of the mixture onto it.

5 Hang the shelf from the 3rd runners in the roasting oven and bake for about 7 – 10 minutes until puffed up and golden.

6 You will need to do this in several batches, the biscuits spread as they cook!

7 Cool the biscuits on a wire rack.

blackberry chutney

Makes 6 jars

2lb /1kg cooking apples

1lb (450g) onions

10 oz (275g) caster sugar

¼ pint (150ml) balsamic vinegar

2 tsp ground cinnamon

Several grinds of black pepper

1 lb (450g) blackberries

Oven:

Simmering oven

Prepare in advance:

Keeps for up to a year

Freeze:

No need

1   Wash six jam jars and put them, still wet, into the simmering oven to sterilise.

2   Quarter the apples and remove the cores, then chop them into a large pan.

3   Peel and slice the onions and put them into the pan, together with the sugar, vinegar, cinnamon and pepper.

4   Put a lid onto the pan and set it on the simmering plate to heat up. When it is boiling and the lid too hot to rest your hand on, transfer to the simmering oven for an hour.

5   Move the pan back to the simmering plate, then add the blackberries. Re-cover and put back into the simmering oven for another 20 minutes.

6   The chutney should now be thick and soft, so tip it into a jug, and then into the hot jars. Seal with cling film and a lid whilst still hot. Label the jars!

7   The chutney should be ready to eat within a week, because of the sweet vinegar. Or it will happily sit in a cupboard for a year.

grape and apple pickle

Makes 6 jars

2lb (1kg) apples

12 oz (375g) seedless grapes

3 onions

1 lb (450g) light brown sugar

¾ pint (450ml) cider vinegar

1 tsp ground cumin

1 tsp ground coriander

1 tsp mustard seeds

1" (2½ cm) piece fresh ginger

2 cloves garlic

1 tsp salt

2 red chillies (optional!)

Oven:

Simmering oven, 130C, 250F, Gas
1 and floor of roasting oven

Prepare in advance:

Pickle will keep for up to a year in
the larder

Freeze:

No need

1 Peel, core and chop the apples, peel and chop the
onions, chop the chillies if using and crush the garlic.
Peel and grate the ginger.

2 Tip all the ingredients into a large pan and bring to
the boil on the boiling plate.

3 Cover and transfer the pan to the simmering oven for
about two hours, until the fruit is soft, then remove
the lid of the pan and stir the contents.

4 Wash six jam jars and put them, still wet, into the
simmering oven to sterilise.

5 Put the pan onto the floor of the roasting oven to boil,
thicken and reduce for about 30–45 minutes.

6 Stir the pickle and pour it into sterilised jars. Seal,
label and leave to cool.

Aga tip: Seal the jars with some plastic film between the jar and the metal lid, to prevent
the vinegar in the pickle from corroding the metal lid

jim's legendary tomato and chilli sauce

To feed more people: Make double!

Makes about ¾ pint, 2 smallish jars

2lb fresh or 1 tin tomatoes

2 red chillies

2 cloves garlic

1 tsp smoked paprika

2 tbsp red wine vinegar

2 tbsp caster sugar

1 tsp salt

1 tsp cornflour

Oven:

Simmering plate, floor of roasting oven

Prepare in advance:

Keeps for months in a sterilised jar

Freeze:

No need

1 Tip all the ingredients into a food processor and whizz until smooth.

2 Pour into a saucepan and cook, either the simmering plate or on the floor of the roasting oven for about 15 minutes until darkened and thick. Stir occasionally.

3 Pour the sauce into sterilised jars, seal and label.

red onion conserve

Makes two jars

6 red onions

3 tbsp balsamic vinegar

3 tbsp water

1 tsp mustard seeds

1 tsp cardamom seeds

Oven:

Simmering oven, 130C, 250F,
Gas 1

Prepare in advance:

The conserve will keep in a sealed
jar for months

1   Peel and chop the onions.

2   Crush the mustard seeds and cardamom seeds in a
pestle and mortar.

3   Put all the ingredients into a pan and bring to the boil
on the simmering plate.

4   Cover and transfer to the simmering oven for three
hours.

5   Tip into sterilised jars and seal.

cheats hollandaise sauce

Every time I make this sauce I think of my friend Kate, who has used this method for years with far more success than I ever did when whizzing it in the processor

Serves 4

2 egg yolks

½ tsp balsamic vinegar *or* 1 tsp lemon juice

4 oz (110g) butter

Salt and pepper

Oven:

Simmering plate

Prepare ahead:

Keep beside the Aga for up to an hour

Freeze:

No

1 Put the butter into a pan and set onto the simmering plate to melt.

2 Put the yolks into a bowl, with the balsamic vinegar or lemon juice and seasoning.

3 Bring the butter to the boil. Whisk the yolk mixture with an electric whisk, then pour on the boiling butter in a steady stream, whisking all the time.

4 The sauce will thicken magically as the butter emulsifies and cooks the yolks.

5 To keep the sauce warm before serving, cover with cling film and set on the side of the Aga on a folded tea towel to stop it from getting too hot and curdling whilst you are not looking!

sofrito — spanish tomato sauce

10 ripe plum tomatoes

2 red peppers

¼ pint (150ml) rapeseed oil

4 small onions

1 teaspoon sugar

1 teaspoon salt

1 teaspoon smoked paprika

2 to 3 bay leaves

Oven:

Simmering oven, 130C, 250F,
Gas 1 and floor of roasting oven

Prepare in advance:

Cooked cooled sauce will keep in
the fridge for 24 hours

Prepare ahead:

Will keep warm in the simmering
or warming oven for an hour

Freeze:

Yes

1   Cut the tomatoes and peppers into chunks. Peel and chop the onions. If you are feeling really keen, scald and peel the tomatoes and remove the seeds.

2   Heat the oil in a medium saucepan and add the onions, sugar and salt. Cover with a tight fitting lid and when the lid is too hot to leave your hand on, move the pan to the simmering oven for 40 to 45 minutes, until the onions are tender and lightly caramelised.

3   Add the chopped tomatoes and peppers and any juices, the smoked paprika and bay leaves; mix well. Move the pan to the floor of the roasting oven and cook, uncovered, for 15 minutes.

4   Remove the bay leaves before serving or storing (leave to cool before storing).

heart attack sauce

To feed more people: Double the quantity will feed up to 10, depending how much you put on each plate!

Serves 4

½ pint (300ml) double cream

¼ pint (150ml) cold pressed rapeseed oil or olive oil if you prefer

4 cloves garlic

Large sprig fresh rosemary

2 bay leaves

Salt and pepper

Oven:

Simmering plate and simmering oven, 130C, 250F, Gas 1

Prepare in advance:

Will keep in the fridge for 2 days

Prepare ahead:

Will keep warm on the back of the Aga for a couple of hours

Freeze:

Yes, freeze in small portions to add to mashed potato etc.

1   Slice the garlic cloves.

2   Put all the ingredients into a pan and bring to the boil.

3   Transfer the pan, without a lid, to the simmering oven and leave it simmering for about half an hour.

4   Strain, then season and serve.

Serving suggestions:

- Stir the sauce into mashed potatoes
- Stir the sauce into mashed butter beans
- Pour the sauce over cooked chicken breasts
- Pour the sauce over cooked fish fillets
- Use in place of a standard white sauce in any dish!

custard

Serves 4 – 6 or one very happy person

1 pint (550ml) creamy milk

2 tbsp caster sugar

1 tbsp cornflour

2 egg yolks

Oven:

Aga simmering plate

Prepare ahead:

Cover with cling film and set on
the back of the Aga for up to 1
hour

Freeze:

No

1   Mix the sugar and cornflour with a little milk to form a
paste.

2   Heat the remaining milk in a pan on the simmering
plate, then pour onto the paste, stirring. Return to the
pan and continue to cook on the simmering plate,
stirring until it boils.

3   Remove from the heat and beat in the egg yolks – this
guarantees that they will not curdle in the custard! –
then put into a jug and serve.

aga yogurt

550ml (1 pint) milk

1 tbsp live natural yogurt

Oven:

Simmering plate, simmering oven, 130C, 250F, Gas 1 and back of Aga

Prepare ahead:

Will keep in the fridge for up to 3 days

Freeze:

No

1 Put the milk into a pan and bring to the boil on the simmering plate. Transfer, uncovered, to the simmering oven for 5 minutes for thin yogurt, 30 minutes for thick (Greek-style) yogurt.

2 Remove from the oven and allow to cool to blood temperature. Stir in the live natural yogurt and pour into a dish or jug.

3 Cover with cling film, then stand the jug or dish on a folded tea towel on the back of the Aga. Cover with another folded tea towel and leave for 4 hours or overnight.

4 When the yogurt has thickened and set, cool completely and refrigerate until required.

kate's ginger and
lemon cordial

Forget elderflower cordial, this is a really refreshing drink. Mix the cordial with fizzy water and ice

Makes 2 bottles

6 stalks lemongrass

1 lime

1 lemon

2" (5cms) piece fresh ginger

8 oz (225g) granulated sugar

½ pint (300ml) water

Oven:

Boiling plate

Prepare in advance:

Will keep in the fridge for a week

Freeze:

Yes

1 Bash the lemongrass stalks and put them into a large pan.

2 Grate the rind of the lemon and lime into the pan, then squeeze in the juice.

3 Wash and slice the ginger into the pan, then add the sugar and water.

4 Bring to the boil on the boiling plate then transfer to the simmering plate and simmer for about 10 minutes.

5 Pour into sterilised bottles and seal.

Aga tip: To sterilise bottles and jam jars: wash thoroughly then put, still wet, into a roasting tin. Put the tin into the simmering oven for about 15 minutes until the jars are dry and sterile. Don't forget to sterilise the lids too!

index